A Note From Rick Renner

I am on a personal quest to see a " the Bible" so people can establish their lives on a firm foundation that will stand strong and endure the test as the end-time storm winds begin to intensify.

In order to experience a revival of the Bible in your personal life, it is important to take time each day to read, receive, and apply its truths to your life. James tells us that if we will continue in the perfect law of liberty — refusing to be forgetful hearers but determined to be doers — we will be blessed in our ways. As you watch or listen to the programs in this series and work through this corresponding study guide, I trust that you will search the Scriptures and allow the Holy Spirit to help you hear something new from God's Word that applies specifically to your life. I encourage you to be a doer of the Word that He reveals to you. Whatever the cost, I assure you — it will be worth it.

> Thy words were found, and I did eat them;
> and thy word was unto me the joy and rejoicing of mine heart:
> for I am called by thy name, O Lord God of hosts.
> — Jeremiah 15:16

Your brother and friend in Jesus Christ,

Rick Renner

Why We Need the Gifts of the Holy Spirit

Copyright © 2021 by Rick Renner
8316 E. 73rd St.
Tulsa, Oklahoma 74133

Published by Rick Renner Ministries
www.renner.org

ISBN 13: 978-1-6803-1593-6

eBook ISBN 13: 978-1-6803-1631-5

How To Use This Study Guide

This ten-lesson study guide corresponds to *"Why We Need the Gifts of the Holy Spirit" With Rick Renner* (**Renner TV**). Each lesson in this study guide covers a topic that is addressed during the program series, with questions and references supplied to draw you deeper into your own private study of the Scriptures on this subject.

To derive the most benefit from this study guide, consider the following:

First, watch or listen to the program prior to working through the corresponding lesson in this guide. (Programs can also be viewed at **renner.org** by clicking on the Media/Archives links.)

Second, take the time to look up the scriptures included in each lesson. Prayerfully consider their application to your own life.

Third, use a journal or notebook to make note of your answers to each lesson's Study Questions and Practical Application challenges.

Fourth, invest specific time in prayer and in the Word of God to consult with the Holy Spirit. Write down the scriptures or insights He reveals to you.

Finally, take action! Whatever the Lord tells you to do according to His Word, do it.

For added insights on this subject, it is recommended that you obtain Rick Renner's book *Why We Need the Gifts of the Holy Spirit*. You may also select from Rick's other available resources by placing your order at **renner.org** or by calling 1-800-742-5593.

TOPIC
The Move of the Holy Spirit in Corinth

SCRIPTURES
1 Corinthians 6:9-11 — Know ye not that the unrighteous shall not inherit the kingdom of God? Be not deceived: neither fornicators, nor idolaters, nor adulterers, nor effeminate, nor abusers of themselves with mankind, nor thieves, nor covetous, nor drunkards, nor revilers, nor extortioners, shall inherit the kingdom of God. And such were some of you....

GREEK WORDS
There are no Greek words in this lesson.

SYNOPSIS
The ten lessons in this study on *Why We Need the Gifts of the Holy Spirit* will focus on the following topics:

- The Move of the Holy Spirit in Corinth
- The Eruptive Power of God in Corinth
- The Enriching of Spiritual Gifts
- The Supernatural Confirmation of the Holy Spirit
- Why We Need the Gifts of the Holy Spirit
- The Gifts of the Holy Spirit, Part 1
- The Gifts of the Holy Spirit, Part 2
- Making Room for Spiritual Gifts
- The Need To Do Things Decently and in Order
- The Church of Corinth: A Divine Pattern or an Anomaly?

The emphasis of this lesson:

The gifts of the Holy Spirit moved mightily in the church in Corinth. Rather than cause the people to act carnal, the gifts served to bring the issues of carnality and sin to the surface so that they could be dealt with and the believers could mature in Christ.

Saint Isaac's Cathedral is located in Saint Petersburg, Russia, and its foundation was first laid in 1818 by Emperor Alexander I just after his victory over Napoleon. It took 40 years to construct this magnificent cathedral, which consists of more than 300,000 tons of materials. Workers used 20 different kinds of stone from Russia and all over Europe, including 16 tons of malachite and 1,100 pounds of deep blue lapis.

The interior of this shrine is simply spectacular. You might say the inside of Saint Isaac's Cathedral looks like an explosion of opulence and splendor. The ornamentation, the paintings, and the mosaics are just bursting with vibrant color. In the same way, the church in Corinth was an explosion of the Holy Spirit's power. The gifts and manifestations of the Spirit there were innumerable. Indeed, it was a *church* like no other in a *city* like no other, and there are many things we can learn from how God moved in this congregation.

Many Churches Today Are Closed To the Manifestation of the Gifts

When Rick was growing up, he attended a wonderful church. But as lovely as so many of the experiences were in his church, one crucial element was missing — *the gifts of the Holy Spirit*. They did not believe in the present-day manifestation of the Holy Spirit. The official position of the denomination he was a part of was that the gifts of the Spirit had been a part of the Early Church in its formative years, but they had passed away with the death of the apostles. Doctrinally, they were what we would call *cessationists*, which is taken from the word *cease*, meaning *to come to an end*.

Many churches today fall into the category of *cessationists*. They lean heavily on the intellectual study of Scripture and want nothing to do with any kind of supernatural displays. In fact, because these churches don't believe in the manifestations of spiritual gifts in this present day, they often deem Pentecostals and Charismatics to be doctrinally off-base. They dismiss the demonstrations of the Holy Spirit as immature nonsense — silly people doing fleshly things. What is equally disheartening is that while a great number of Pentecostal and charismatic churches today doctrinally believe in the gifts of the Spirit, they do not experience them in manifestation. For some churches, the reason for this is the fear of offending attenders, and for other churches it is the drive to maintain a tight time schedule that leaves no room for the Spirit to move.

Some denominations go so far as to teach that the gifts of the Holy Spirit are what made the church in Corinth childish and carnal. It's true that the church in Corinth was carnal. In fact, it is considered to be the most carnal church in the Early New Testament era. But was their carnality a result of the working of the Holy Spirit? Would God actually give spiritual gifts to cause people to be immature and carnal? Of course not. The Holy Spirit is never the source of immaturity and carnality.

A survey of the New Testament and early Christian history shows that all the churches of the First Century had problems with carnality. At that time, most Christians were getting saved out of a pagan world filled with immorality, drunkenness, and carnality of every type. Early converts carried much of that old baggage into their new life in Christ. That is the reason Paul had to instruct the churches in all his letters on how to deal with and overcome various issues of carnality. Even the more mature church of Ephesus seemed to have had a problem with drunkenness (*see* Ephesians 5:18). So why is the Corinthian church often portrayed as being the most carnal of all New Testament churches?

THE HISTORY OF CORINTH

It Was Known for Its Rebellion and Founded by the Rude and Crude of Society

To help you get a better understanding of why the church in Corinth has been labeled the most carnal church of Early New Testament times, let's take a look at a little of the history of the city of Corinth itself. Historical information helps explain why this particular church had so many difficult issues.

Corinth was a very ancient city that had previously rebelled against the authority of Rome. As a result, Rome attacked and utterly destroyed the city in 146 BC, and it laid in ruins and was uninhabited for nearly a hundred years. There was nothing left but a pile of rubble. Then in 44 BC, Julius Caesar decided to reestablish Corinth as a Roman colony.

Geographically, it had an advantageous position on the narrow Greek isthmus that served as a "land bridge" to link central and southern Greece. But rebuilding Corinth was a challenge because not many people wanted to relocate to an old, devastated pile of ruins. So to lure people to move to Corinth and help rebuild, Julius Caesar offered the incentive of a new life to veteran Roman legionnaires (veteran soldiers) as well as to the poor and freed slaves of Rome. Caesar promised free land to those who relocated to Corinth to help reconstruct it, and they would also become the new city's leaders.

This was an opportunity that these people would never have anywhere else. As a result of this offer, large numbers of people — former soldiers, sailors, veterans, poor people, and freed slaves — moved to Corinth, and they became the founding fathers of the new city. This was a foul, crude, and carnal group — to say the least — and they formed the moral foundation for the new city.

Corinth Was Home to a Thriving Sex Industry

Along with the lewd, crude, and rude bunch that founded the city, the goddess Aphrodite was the prominent deity in the old Corinth. What's interesting is that Julius Caesar — who ordered the city to be rebuilt — believed he was a direct descendent of Aphrodite. So he dedicated the new city of Corinth to the goddess Aphrodite. Since Aphrodite was the goddess of sex and of prostitutes, the sex industry played a major role in the reconstructed city.

A significant temple was built to the worship of Aphrodite on top of the Acrocorinth, which was the large hill that overshadowed the city, and multiple additional temples were erected to this goddess throughout Corinth. These temples allowed the sex industry to flourish. No doubt the large population of lower-class freed slaves and tough legionnaires were given to the sex trade. And in addition to the large volume of local patronage, Corinth became known as a place people could experience sex vacations.

Keep in mind, the city was located exactly between two ports: the port on the west coast received ships from Rome, and the port on the east coast received ships from Asia. People came in droves to indulge themselves in the flesh feast that freely flowed in Corinth. The city's thriving sex industry put it on the map as a major tourist stop for sailors and travelers who made their way into Corinth to treat themselves to sexual pleasures.

Drunkenness, Rivalry, and Thievery Abounded

Additionally, Corinth was also widely known for its culture of drunken debauchery. The excessive use of alcohol by Corinthians was so notorious that if a person lived in the Roman world and was a drunkard, it is likely that person would have been referred to as a "Corinthian." In fact, Corinth's reputation for drunkenness was so bad that the term "to corinthianize" came to refer to anyone engaging in any form of debauchery — sexual sins as well as drunkenness.

When it came to theatrical performances, drunken actors were always portrayed as Corinthians. This was the reputation of Corinthians across the Roman world. They were generally thought of as lower-class, crude, fornicating drunkards.

Furthermore, not far from Corinth was a smaller city that featured a large stadium where the Panhellenic Games of ancient Greece were held every two years. Because Corinth was the city closest to these games, it became the official host city of these sports events and benefited from revenue generated from people who came from all over the Roman world to either participate in or view the games.

The large number of visitors who stayed in Corinth contributed to the growth of the sex industry, the increased sale of alcohol, and to the tourist business in general. Moreover, the Panhellenic Games were highly competitive events, and as a result a spirit of rivalry and competition affected the mindset of Corinthians. This marked the city as a place of *fierce competition*. In fact, the rivalry was so great, a spirit of competition even made its way into the church in Corinth. We read about this in chapter 1 of First Corinthians.

Add to this one more element — *thievery*. Because Corinth was filled with tourists wanting to get drunk and pamper their sexual appetite, as well as people seeking a new future, it also attracted fortune hunters who wanted to make a quick and easy buck. These professional swindlers and con artists saw this as a great opportunity to make fast money, so they, too, arrived in large numbers.

If you mix all these elements together, it paints a clear picture of First Century Corinth. It was a city where…

- The founding fathers consisted of immoral soldiers and sailors, freed slaves, and the poor.
- Unrestricted sex and limitless consumption of alcohol was celebrated.
- A fierce spirit of competition reigned.
- Swindlers, charlatans, and cheaters abounded.

When all these ingredients are in one place and all restraint is thrown to the wind, it results in a city like Corinth. These were the kind of people who got saved under Paul's ministry and made up the church in Corinth.

The Corinthian Believers Had a Very Carnal Past

Paul described who the Corinthians were before they came to Christ in First Corinthians 6:9-11, saying,

> Know ye not that the unrighteous shall not inherit the kingdom of God? Be not deceived: neither fornicators, nor idolaters, nor adulterers, nor effeminate, nor abusers of themselves with mankind, nor thieves, nor covetous, nor drunkards, nor revilers, nor extortioners, shall inherit the kingdom of God. And such were some of you….

Clearly, this church was full of individuals with a morally lurid past. This explains why there was so much carnality in the Corinthian Church. Believers there were still dealing with sexual sin, alcohol abuse, competition among themselves, and taking advantage of one another. It was because of their rough and tough background that Paul wrote them in such a strong and direct manner compared to the way he addressed other congregations. The Corinthians were raised in a culture known for its coarseness, so Paul communicated to them in a manner they would understand and respond to.

To be clear, the carnality in the church in Corinth had nothing to do with the gifts of the Holy Spirit. It had to do with the carnal environment from which the people in the church had been saved. On the surface, it "appeared" that the Corinthian Church had more problems than other churches. But their issues were a result of how they lived *before* they came to Christ. These believers were still in the process of overcoming and learning to live transformed lives.

The amazing thing is that in spite of the carnality of the Corinthians, God moved mightily among them. Because their hearts were open to the truth, God poured out His grace in Corinth, and when that grace showed up, the people experienced the mighty eruptive power of God.

The Gifts of the Spirit
Were Instruments of Cleansing

The fact is, the gifts of the Holy Spirit brought the issues in the people to the surface. Blatant sin, wrong attitudes, carnality, and flaws were all revealed as the gifts of the Holy Spirit manifested. Sin that might stay hidden below the surface in other churches could not remain hidden in Corinth, because the revelatory gifts of the Spirit ensured it would be exposed and cleansed. The operation of these gifts served as God's instrument to bring conviction and correction and reveal what needed to be changed.

The apostle Paul teaches clearly we need the gifts of the Holy Spirit because they bring the presence of Christ right into the church. It is the gifts of the Holy Spirit that establish us in our understanding of Jesus, and when they begin to operate among us, it supernaturally enables us to partner with Jesus and brings us into fellowship with God on a very practical, spiritual level.

Friend, if carnality eliminates someone from being used by God, the church in Corinth would have indeed been eliminated. But that was not the case. The Spirit of God moved mightily in Corinth, and if He could move in the gifts of the Holy Spirit in Corinth, then He can move in the gifts of the Spirit in any church. All we need is an open heart and mind.

STUDY QUESTIONS

Study to shew thyself approved unto God, a workman that needeth not to be ashamed, rightly dividing the word of truth.
— 2 Timothy 2:15

1. What new insights did you learn about the city of Corinth's history and its people? What details were most surprising about Corinth's founding and what the city was known for?

2. In what ways would you say Corinth is a lot like many of the major cities in America? How does the birth of the church in Corinth give you hope for God to birth a miracle in your city and country?

PRACTICAL APPLICATION

But be ye doers of the word, and not hearers only,
deceiving your own selves.
—James 1:22

1. What have you been taught about the gifts of the Holy Spirit? Were you told that they ceased with the death of the apostles, or that they are still operating in the Church today?

2. Are the gifts of the Holy Spirit operating in the church *you* attend? Are they operating in *your life*? If so, which ones have you experienced? If the gifts are not operating in your life, why?

LESSON 2

TOPIC

The Eruptive Power of God in Corinth

SCRIPTURES

1. **1 Corinthians 2:4** — And my speech and my preaching was not with enticing words of man's wisdom, but in demonstration of the Spirit and of power.

2. **2 Corinthians 12:12** — Truly the signs of an apostle were wrought among you in all patience, in signs, and wonders, and mighty deeds.

3. **1 Corinthians 1:4-7** — I thank my God always on your behalf, for the grace of God which is given you by Jesus Christ; that in every thing ye are enriched by him, in all utterance, and in all knowledge; even as the testimony of Christ was confirmed in you: So that ye

come behind in no gift; waiting for the coming of our Lord Jesus Christ.

GREEK WORDS

1. "demonstration"— ἀπόδειξις (*apodeiksis*): to point at something; to draw attention to a thing; to point at an object; to show off; to demonstrate; to display

2. "power"— δύναμις (*dunamis*): power; explosive, superhuman power that comes with enormous energy and produces phenomenal, extraordinary, and unparalleled results; a force of nature like a hurricane, tornado, or earthquake; the full, advancing force of an army; power that is impressive, incomparable, and beyond human ability to perform; miraculous power or miraculous manifestations

3. "signs"— σημεῖον (*semeion*): a sign that verifies or authenticates a thing; used in the Gospels primarily to depict miracles and supernatural events that were intended to verify and authenticate the message of the Gospel

4. "wonders"— τέρας (*teras*): an event that leaves one baffled, bewildered, astonished, at a loss for words; depicts the shock, surprise, or astonishment felt by bystanders who observed events that were contrary to the normal course of nature; miraculous events that left spectators speechless, shocked, astonished, bewildered, baffled, taken aback, stunned, awestruck, and in a state of wonder

5. "mighty deeds"— δύναμις (*dunamis*) power; explosive, superhuman power that comes with enormous energy and produces phenomenal, extraordinary, and unparalleled results; a force of nature like a hurricane, tornado, or earthquake; the full, advancing force of an army; power that is impressive, incomparable, and beyond human ability to perform; miraculous power or miraculous manifestations

6. "grace"— χάρις (*charis*): denoted a special touch conferred upon an individual or group of individuals by the gods; once χάρις (*charis*) was conferred upon a person or group of people, it imparted to them superhuman abilities; it enabled them to do what they could not normally or naturally do; it always comes with outward evidence or visible manifestation; in some literature, the word χάρις (*charis*) was even used to denote individuals who had been placed under a "magic spell" that transformed their personalities and imparted supernatural abilities to them; in the New Testament, the word χάρις (*charis*) is

occasionally translated as "favor" because a person who receives *charis* has been supernaturally enabled as a result of receiving a manifestation of favor from God

SYNOPSIS

As we have seen, Saint Isaac's Cathedral in Saint Petersburg, Russia, is simply magnificent in beauty, and it served as the central cathedral for the entire Russian Empire for nearly half a century. Its interior is lavishly adorned with marvelous mosaics, massive paintings, and 881 pounds of gold. The inside perimeter of the cathedral is surrounded with magnificent columns and pillars, each embellished with Corinthian capitals.

These Corinthian capitals, which were exquisitely carved and covered in gold, bring to mind the amazing city of Corinth itself. It is the city where the apostle Paul met his ministry partners Aquila and Priscilla, and together they founded the thriving church of Corinth — a church where the power of the Holy Spirit erupted for decades on end.

What was it about the church in Corinth that enabled them to openly embrace and experience the power of God? What can we learn from this group of believers and apply in our lives today to witness a fresh outpouring of the gifts of the Holy Spirit?

The emphasis of this lesson:

When Paul arrived in Corinth, he came with a visible demonstration of the Holy Spirit's power, not just an intellectual presentation of the Gospel. Through Paul, God performed signs, wonders, and mighty deeds. He poured out His grace upon the church in Corinth, and it visibly manifested in the gifts of the Holy Spirit operating mightily among them.

How the Gospel First Came to Corinth

The apostle Paul wrote letters to many of the churches he helped to plant on his missionary journeys. Two of these letters were to the church in Corinth, and they're included as books of the Bible. In First Corinthians 2:4, Paul wrote about how he ministered to the people when he first arrived in Corinth. He said, "And my speech and my preaching was not with enticing words of man's wisdom, but in demonstration of the Spirit and of power."

Notice the word "demonstration" in this verse. It is the Greek word *apodeiksis*, and it means *to point at something; to draw attention to a thing*, or *to point at an object*. It could also be translated *to show off; to demonstrate*; or *to display*. The use of this word indicates that when Paul showed up in Corinth, he came with a visible demonstration of the Holy Spirit's power. Although there is value in studying and speaking words of wisdom that engage the mind, Paul knew from experience that an intellectual presentation of the Gospel alone was not enough. He had just done that in the city of Athens, and it yielded very little fruit. A clear demonstration of the power of God is what was needed, and that's what Paul and his ministry team brought with them.

Another important word in First Corinthians 2:4 is the word "power," which in Greek is the well-known word *dunamis*. It describes *explosive, superhuman power that comes with enormous energy and produces phenomenal, extraordinary, and unparalleled results*. It's a force of nature like a hurricane, tornado, or an earthquake. This word *dunamis* was also used to denote *the full, advancing force of an army*. This *dunamis* power is impressive, incomparable, and beyond human ability to perform. In the New Testament, it primarily depicted miraculous power or miraculous manifestations.

Thus, the big difference between Paul's ministry in Athens and his ministry in Corinth was his decision to make room for the Holy Spirit to move and manifest His power. Rather than just provide intellectual information, Paul made room for God's supernatural demonstration. Indeed, God showed up and showed off His *dunamis* power! It was *explosive, superhuman power that came with enormous energy and produced phenomenal, extraordinary, and unparalleled results*. Likewise, if we want to see the *dunamis* power of the Holy Spirit move in our lives and in our churches, we have to make room for Him to move.

God Performed 'Signs, Wonders, and Mighty Deeds'

When we come to Paul's second letter to the Corinthian believers, we see him testify once more as to what took place when he first began to preach the Gospel among them. Paul wrote, "Truly the signs of an apostle were wrought among you in all patience, in signs, and wonders, and mighty deeds" (2 Corinthians 12:12). Paul declared that three types of supernatural demonstrations took place when he ministered: *signs, wonders*, and *mighty deeds*.

(handwritten note: Healing the sick/lame)

The word "signs" in Greek is the word *semeion*, which describes *a sign that verifies or authenticates a thing*. This word is used in the Gospels primarily to depict *miracles* and *supernatural events* that were intended to verify and authenticate the message of the Gospel.

The word "wonders" is the Greek word *teras*, and it describes *an event that leaves one baffled, bewildered, astonished,* or *at a loss for words*. It depicts the shock, surprise, or astonishment felt by bystanders who observed events that were contrary to the normal course of nature. These were miraculous events that left spectators speechless, shocked, astonished, bewildered, baffled, taken aback, stunned, awestruck, and in a state of wonder. That's what the people in Corinth experienced under the ministry of Paul.

(handwritten margin notes: multiply food — cast demons into swine)

In addition to "signs" and "wonders," the Bible says Paul also performed "mighty deeds." Interestingly, the words "mighty deeds" are a translation of the Greek word *dunamis* — the same word that's translated as "power" in First Corinthians 2:4. Again, it describes *explosive, superhuman power that comes with enormous energy and produces phenomenal, extraordinary, and unparalleled results.* It is the very word used by the Greeks to illustrate a force of nature like a hurricane, tornado, or earthquake. It is also the exact word used to denote *the full, advancing force of an army* that drove out enemy invaders. The "mighty deeds" done by Paul were displays of power that were impressive, incomparable, and beyond human ability to perform. Indeed, they were miraculous manifestations. *(handwritten: Luke ??)*

Again, Paul did not solely rely on sharing intellectual information. He made a decision in his heart to make room for God to supernaturally move in the midst of the people. Sure enough, God showed up and confirmed that Paul's message was true by authenticating it with signs, wonders, and mighty deeds. This means the church in Corinth was born in the power of the Spirit. God's grace had been liberally poured out on these carnal converts, and He was changing their lives in amazing ways.

(handwritten: – But they needed the foundation)

A Historical Understanding of the Word 'Grace'

As Paul opened his first letter to the Corinthians, he wrote, "I thank my God always on your behalf, for the grace of God which is given you by Jesus Christ; that in every thing ye are enriched by him, in all utterance, and in all knowledge; even as the testimony of Christ was confirmed in you: So that ye come behind in no gift; waiting for the coming of our Lord Jesus Christ" (1 Corinthians 1:4-7). Once more, Paul speaks of the grace of God being given to the Corinthian believers, and that grace came in the form of an explosion of spiritual gifts within the church.

One of the most important words to understand in this passage is the word *grace*. There is a great deal of talk and teaching on the subject of *grace*, but in order to accurately grasp what it means, we need to have an understanding of the historical context of where the word *grace* came from.

The word "grace" is the Greek word *charis*, and it originally denoted *a special touch conferred upon an individual or group of individuals by the gods*. Once *charis* — "grace" — was conferred upon a person or group of people, it imparted to them superhuman abilities. That touch of "grace" enabled them to do what they could not normally or naturally do, and it *always* came with outward evidence or visible manifestation. Hence, you could always see the effects of grace on a person.

In some ancient literature, the word *charis* (grace) was even used to denote individuals who had been placed under a "magic spell" that transformed their personalities and imparted supernatural abilities to them. People were known to say, "Oh, that person's under a spell — that person is under grace (*charis*). They are operating under some type of divine influence, which has changed them and given them abilities that they didn't naturally possess."

In the New Testament, the word *charis* is occasionally translated as "favor," because it depicts a favorable touch that an individual did not earn or deserve. It was a manifestation of favor from God freely bestowed upon that person, and once he or she received it, that person was supernaturally enabled to do things he or she could not previously do.

God's Grace Is a Divine Impartation That Enables, Empowers, and Strengthens

So when we read about "grace" in the apostle Paul's writings, he was always referring to God graciously imparting a special touch that *enables*, *empowers*, and *strengthens* the recipient. It's a deposit of divine power that transforms and gives one superhuman abilities *to be* and *to do* what he could not be or do before. A person or group of people would never experience *charis* (grace) without some type of *outward evidence* or *demonstration.* Thus, grace is *never* silent or invisible. When it shows up in an individual or a church, it is undeniable.

Of course, God's grace first produces *inward change*, but it always comes with *outward evidence*. In the case of the Corinthians, when God's grace touched them, it became visible by the gifts of the Holy Spirit that operated mightily among them. Specifically, grace manifested in the form of spiritual gifts of utterance and gifts of knowledge (*see* 1 Corinthians 1:5).

In the same way, if you have been touched by God's grace, you should *expect* grace to visibly show up in areas of your life. Grace enables you to be what you previously could never be and empowers you to do what you naturally could never do. It causes a normal, natural human being to be able to operate in the supernatural. Again, Paul teaches one byproduct of this divine impartation of grace is the overflowing operation of the Holy Spirit's gifts in the life of a believer or a church. And God's grace *always* comes with an outward evidence or visible demonstration.

In our next lesson, we'll continue to look at First Corinthians 1:4-9 and see how the gifts of the Holy Spirit make you spiritually rich.

STUDY QUESTIONS

> **Study to shew thyself approved unto God, a workman that needeth not to be ashamed, rightly dividing the word of truth.**
> **— 2 Timothy 2:15**

Visible to others as supernatural ability to do what cannot be done naturally or normally

1. Prior to this lesson, what was your understanding of the *grace* of God? Taking what you learned about the historical meaning of *grace*, how has your understanding of God's *grace* been illuminated and enlarged?

2. The New Testament has much to say about God's *grace*. Take a few moments to look up these key passages and describe what they say about receiving the grace of God in your life.
   - Psalm 84:11 — *God bestows favor/honor - No good thing does He withhold from the upright*
   - James 4:6; 1 Peter 5:5,6 — *God gives grace to the humble*
   - 2 Corinthians 9:8

God is able to make all grace abound to you

So That

Having all sufficiency in all things at all times (every single thing you need whenever you need it)

You may abound in every good work

Why We Need the Gifts of the Holy Spirit | 17

PRACTICAL APPLICATION

**But be ye doers of the word, and not hearers only,
deceiving your own selves.
— James 1:22**

1. Have you ever personally witnessed the *dunamis* power of the Holy Spirit moving in your life or the life of your church? What did it look like? What *signs, wonders,* or *mighty deeds* took place? How did the Spirit's *extraordinary, unparalleled* manifestations increase your faith?

2. In what areas of your life can you see the divine touch of God's grace (*charis*) operating? What is the outward evidence or visible demonstration? In what other areas do you need to pray and ask God to pour out His grace — so that you can begin to do what you cannot normally or naturally do?

3. The big difference between Paul's ministry in Athens and in Corinth was his decision to make room for the Holy Spirit to move and manifest His power. How are you making room for the Holy Spirit to display His power in *your life*? In *your church*? In *your family*? In *your community*? If you don't know what to do, pray and ask the Holy Spirit to give you some practical steps you can take to help create an environment where He feels welcome to move.

LESSON 3

TOPIC

The Enriching of Spiritual Gifts

SCRIPTURES

1. **1 Corinthians 12:4** — Now there are diversities of gifts, but the same Spirit.

2. **1 Corinthians 12:8-10** — For to one is given by the Spirit the word of wisdom; to another the word of knowledge by the same Spirit; To another faith by the same Spirit; to another the gifts of healing by the same Spirit; To another the working of miracles; to another prophecy; to another discerning of spirits; to another divers kinds of tongues; to another the interpretation of tongues.

3. **1 Corinthians 1:4,5** — I thank my God always on your behalf, for the grace of God which is given you by Jesus Christ; That in every thing ye are enriched by him, in all utterance, and in all knowledge.

4. **1 Corinthians 15:10** — But by the grace of God I am what I am: and his grace which was bestowed upon me was not in vain; but I laboured more abundantly than they all: yet not I, but the grace of God which was with me.

5. **Romans 8:17** — And if children, then heirs; heirs of God, and joint-heirs with Christ.

GREEK WORDS

1. "grace" — **χάρις** (*charis*): denoted a special touch conferred upon an individual or group of individuals by the gods; once **χάρις** (*charis*) was conferred upon a person or group of people, it imparted to them superhuman abilities; it enabled them to do what they could not normally or naturally do; it always comes with outward evidence or visible manifestation; in some literature, the word **χάρις** (*charis*) was even used to denote individuals who had been placed under a "magic spell" that transformed their personalities and imparted supernatural abilities to them; in the New Testament, the word **χάρις** (*charis*) is occasionally translated as "favor" because a person who receives charis has been supernaturally enabled as a result of receiving a manifestation of favor from God

2. "but" — **δὲ** (*de*): however, consequently; emphatic statement

3. "bestowed upon me" — **εἰς ἐμὲ** (*eis eme*): into me; toward me; movement toward me

4. "vain" — **κενός** (*kenos*): empty; hollow; ineffective; vain; profitless; worthless

5. "with" — **σὺν** (*sun*): with; implying partnership

6. "every thing" — **ἐν παντὶ** (*en panti*): in every way; in every respect

7. "enriched" — **πλουτίζω** (*ploutidzo*): wealth so great it cannot be tabulated; abundant wealth; vast wealth; extreme riches; incredible abundance; magnificent opulence; extravagant lavishness; used by Plato to say no one was richer than legendary King Midas

8. "by" — **ἐν** (*en*): in or by

9. "joint-heirs" — **συγκληρονόμος** (*sunkleronomos*): a co-inheritor; a joint-heir

SYNOPSIS

As we've noted, Saint Isaac's Cathedral in Saint Petersburg, Russia, is filled with beauty beyond description. The main altar inside this church is made up of 16 tons of malachite that artists painstakingly arranged piece by tiny piece to form a marvelous mosaic. There are also 1,100 pounds of deep blue lapis used in the decorations of this altar, all of which came from the land of Afghanistan. In all, there are actually 62 intricate mosaics embellishing Saint Isaac's along with 155 massive paintings with depictions of religious figures, and 20 different kinds of exquisite marble from all over the world.

Just as Saint Isaac's is lavishly adorned with opulent treasures, God has embellished the Church with the amazing gifts of the Holy Spirit. The apostle Paul describes these gifts in First Corinthians 12 and explains how they should and should not operate in the Church in First Corinthians 13 and 14. God wants us to understand everything we can about these supernatural gifts so we can experience all the benefits of the Holy Spirit operating in our lives.

The emphasis of this lesson:

The gifts of the Spirit are diverse and vital for the fullness of Christ to be in the Church. It's through God's grace that these spiritual gifts manifested in and through the apostle Paul and the believers in Corinth. Just as the Corinthians were abundantly rich in spiritual gifts, we too are enriched and continue to increase in spiritual wealth as we abide in Christ Jesus.

The Gifts of the Spirit
Are Vital and Varied in the Church

How would you like to have so many spiritual gifts operating in your church that your church was considered to be spiritually wealthy? That's exactly what Paul said was happening in the church in Corinth. Although the believers at Corinth were carnal and had many problems, it did *not* disqualify them from receiving and flowing in the gifts of the Holy Spirit. And if God could manifest His power so greatly in Corinth — where the people struggled with a lot of hang-ups — He can do it anywhere!

Paul taught that the gifts of the Holy Spirit are *vital* for the fullness of Christ to be in the Church. When they are absent, a supernatural element is missing from God's people. And we know that God's plan is for these spiritual manifestations to work in the Church *until* the coming of the Lord Jesus Christ. *word of wisdom, knowledge faith, healing, miracles, prophecy, discernment, Tongues* What's interesting is that in addition to the nine gifts of the Spirit listed in First Corinthians 12:8-10, there are also seven motivational gifts mentioned by the apostle Paul in Romans 12:6-8. These include prophecy, serving, teaching, exhortation, giving, administration, and mercy. Furthermore, the Lord has also given us the five-fold ministry gifts of apostle, prophet, evangelist, pastor, and teacher. These are discussed by Paul in Ephesians 4:11.

In this series, we will focus our attention on the nine gifts of the Holy Spirit Paul wrote about in First Corinthians 12:4,8-10, which says:

> Now there are diversities of gifts, but the same Spirit.… For to one is given by the Spirit the word of wisdom; to another the word of knowledge by the same Spirit; To another faith by the same Spirit; to another the gifts of healing by the same Spirit; To another the working of miracles; to another prophecy; to another discerning of spirits; to another divers kinds of tongues; to another the interpretation of tongues.

These nine gifts are to be operating in your life, in the life of your church, and in the entire Body of Christ. These supernatural endowments — when used in harmony with the leading of the Holy Spirit — produce life and provide dynamic growth to God's people in every way, which is why we need them in operation.

A Review of What Grace Is

In our last lesson, we looked at Paul's words in First Corinthians 1:4, where he said, "I thank my God always on your behalf, for the grace of God which is given you by Jesus Christ." We learned that the word "grace" is extremely important as it is widely used throughout the New Testament. In Greek, the word for "grace" is *charis*, and it is a word that actually originated in the pagan culture.

This word *charis* (grace) denoted *a special touch conferred upon an individual or group of individuals by the gods*. Once *charis* — grace — was granted to a person or group of people, it imparted to them superhuman abilities. That "grace" enabled them to do what they could not normally or naturally do, and it *always* came with outward evidence or visible manifestation. Therefore, when someone had received "grace," it was clearly noticeable.

In some Greek literature, the word *charis* (grace) was even used to denote individuals who had been placed under a "magic spell" that transformed their personalities and imparted supernatural abilities to them. In the New Testament, the word "grace" (*charis*) is occasionally translated as "favor," because it depicts a favorable touch received by an individual or group that did not earn or deserve it. It was a manifestation of favor from God freely bestowed upon them, and once they received it, they were supernaturally enabled to do things they could not do previously.

Paul's words indicate that grace *always* comes with some *outward evidence* or *visible manifestation*, and in the case of the Corinthians, these visible manifestations included an abundance of the gifts of the Holy Spirit. When God poured out His grace on the believers in Corinth, it gave them supernatural abilities they previously did not have. They became spiritually rich because of the grace of God!

Paul Declared His Life and Work Were Solely a Result of God's Grace

Paul recognized the importance and power of God's grace — not only in the lives of others, but also in his own personal life. In First Corinthians 15:10, he declared, "But by the grace of God I am what I am: and his grace which was bestowed upon me was not in vain; but I laboured more abundantly than they all: yet not I, but the grace of God which was with me."

As Paul described the effects of God's grace in a person's life, he begins with the word "but," which is the little Greek word *de*. This word is like an exclamation point for a very emphatic statement being made. It is the equivalent of Paul saying, "But hear me now!"

What was he trying to emphasize so strongly? He said, "By the grace of God I am what I am…" (1 Corinthians 15:10). Here again, we see the word "grace" — the Greek word *charis*, which refers to that *supernatural touch from God that gives us the ability to be and do what we could never be and do on our own.* Hence, the opening of this verse is the same as Paul saying, "I'm not who I used to be; I am totally changed! And the only reason I am who I am today is by the grace (*charis*) of God!"

Paul went on to say that the grace of God was "bestowed upon me." In Greek, this is the phrase *eis eme*, and it indicates *movement*, meaning *toward me*. In other words, God's grace moved toward Paul and was deposited in him, and that grace was not given in "vain." The word "vain" is the Greek word *kenos*, which describes something *empty; hollow; ineffective; vain; profitless;* or *worthless*. Essentially, Paul said, "When the grace of God came into me, it was not wasted. It produced something magnificent inside of me and enabled me to labor more abundantly than everyone else."

To make sure we fully understand where Paul got the ability to do all that he did, he reiterated, "…Yet not I, but the grace of God which was with me" (1 Corinthians 15:10). The word "with" here is the Greek word *sun*, and while it means *with*, it carries the idea of *partnership* and *cooperation*. Friend, when we cooperate with God's grace, it gives us supernatural abilities that are visible and never silent. When grace shows up, it comes with tangible, outward evidence.

Taking into account the original Greek meaning of all these words, we could translate Paul's declaration in First Corinthians 15:10 as him saying, "I am what I am because of the miraculous touch of God's grace on my life! His touch imparted to me abilities that I did not have. I would never be who I am today if God hadn't moved His grace into me and transformed me. As a result of His grace, I'm doing more than anyone else. The abilities I have are amazing, but it's not me. It's God's empowering grace that is partnering with me!"

The Corinthians Were 'Filthy, Stinking Rich' in the Gifts of the Holy Spirit

What else did Paul say about the grace of God given to the Corinthian believers? He said, "That in every thing ye are enriched by him, in all utterance, and in all knowledge" (1 Corinthians 1:5).

The word "every thing" in this verse is a translation of the Greek words *en panti*. The word *panti* is a compound of the word *pan*, meaning *everything*, and the little word *ti*, which describes *the most minute, minuscule detail*. When these words are compounded together, it is the equivalent of saying *in every way* or *in every respect*. Thus, Paul said that *in every way* or *in every respect*, the church in Corinth was enriched by God's grace.

This brings us to the word "enriched" — the Greek word *ploutidzo* — which is an absolutely marvelous word. It describes *wealth so great it cannot be tabulated*. It depicts *abundant wealth; vast wealth; extreme riches; incredible abundance; magnificent opulence;* or *extravagant lavishness*. This word *ploutidzo* is from where we get that word "plutocrat," which refers to *a person who is so rich that he is unable to ascertain the full extent of his own wealth.* It is the very same word used by Plato to describe the riches of the legendary King Midas, whom he declared to be the richest man to ever live up until that time.

The apostle Paul was well-versed in the meaning of the word *ploutidzo.* He used this word in First Corinthians 1:5 to tell the church at Corinth that they were "enriched" by the Lord. That is, they were "filthy stinking rich" when it came to spiritual gifts! And the same is true for *you.* The day you repented of your sins and made Jesus the Lord of your life, you struck it rich. You were supernaturally placed in Christ, and God made you a joint heir with Him (*see* Romans 8:17).

Again, First Corinthians 1:5 says, "…In every thing ye are enriched by him…." The word "by" is the Greek word *en* and can mean either *in him* or *by him*, which conveys two powerful truths to us about the enriching grace of God in our lives. First, the day we were born again and placed *into Jesus Christ* was the richest day of our lives. Second, the Greek word *en* could also emphasize the point that this enrichment process isn't a one-time event — it is an ongoing experience that continues throughout our lives as we walk with God. Hence, this part of the verse could thus be interpreted: "We are enriched as a result of being in Him." Friend, you are invested with great spiritual riches because you are in Him — and that's not all! The longer you remain in Him, the more and more blessed with spiritual wealth you become, and that comes from abiding in relationship with Him.

Gifts of 'Utterance' and 'Knowledge' Abounded

The specific types of riches that Paul described as abounding in the church in Corinth were gifts of "utterance" and the gifts of "knowledge." Utterance — or *vocal gifts* — include tongues, interpretation of tongues, and prophecy. These are spiritual gifts that, when vocalized, supernaturally convey a message from the heart of God to a specific person or congregation. Knowledge — or *revelatory gifts* — include the word of wisdom, the word of knowledge, and discerning of spirits. These are spiritual gifts that supernaturally convey and reveal the heart of God, the hearts of others, or facts and details that naturally could not be known.

It appears that the church in Corinth was *loaded* with these kinds of spiritual gifts. These abilities were in such mighty manifestation that Paul had to write a whole chapter about how to *manage* the huge overflow of spiritual gifts in their assemblies (*see* 1 Corinthians 14).

The Corinthians had been enriched (*ploutidzo*) when they first came to Christ, becoming joint-heirs with Jesus and inheritors of the promises of God. By remaining in Him, they were being made richer in the gifts of the Spirit that operated among them. Based on the meaning of the Greek word *ploutidzo*, you could say the Corinthians were spiritual *plutocrats*. These spiritual gifts were *outward evidences* and *visible manifestations* that showed the grace of God had been liberally poured out on them and that the power of God was operating in their midst.

Friend, the Bible teaches that God is no respecter of persons. Therefore, what God's grace did among the Corinthians is what it will do for every person or church that has a heart to yield to the working of His Spirit in their midst. When God's grace comes upon a person — or on a church — it will always spill over into some type of outward manifestation, *which includes spiritual gifts*. The gifts of the Spirit bring spiritual riches into our lives. The more these gifts operate, the richer we become spiritually!

STUDY QUESTIONS

Study to shew thyself approved unto God, a workman that needeth not to be ashamed, rightly dividing the word of truth.
— 2 Timothy 2:15

It's important to get a glimpse of God's "big picture" regarding the spiritual gifts He has given us. Take a moment to look up these passages and write down the different types of gifts the Holy Spirit manifests in our lives individually and collectively in the Church.

- **The 9 Gifts of the Holy Spirit** — 1 Corinthians 12:8-10 _____
  Wisdom, knowledge word Disern Spicits,
  Faith miracles Healings
  Prophecy Tongues Th terpet

effectively
share
Christ's
gospel
of salvation

- **The 7 Motivational Gifts of the Spirit** — Romans 12:6-8 *Teaching*
  support *Service, Prophecy, Compassion, exhortation, giving, Administer*
- **The Five-fold Ministry Gifts given by Jesus** — Ephesians 4:11 *Teach*
  Apostle, Evangelist Teacher, Prophet, Pastor
  equip • How do you think these three categories of spiritual gifts differ from each other? How do they complement one another?

PRACTICAL APPLICATION

> But be ye doers of the word, and not hearers only,
> deceiving your own selves.
> —James 1:22

1. Paul said, "But by the grace of God I am what I am…" (1 Corinthians 15:10). Looking at your own life, how do you know that it is God's grace and His grace alone that you are who you are today? What has changed in your life that you know only God could change? *Confidence to stand*

2. When it comes to the gifts of the Holy Spirit, how do you see your-self — as spiritually rich or spiritually poor? Which spiritual gifts are operating in your life? How have they enriched you and others?
   wisdom, faith

LESSON 4

TOPIC

The Supernatural Confirmation of the Holy Spirit

SCRIPTURES

1. **1 Corinthians 1:4-6** — I thank my God always on your behalf, for the grace of God which is given you by Jesus Christ; That in every thing ye are enriched by him, in all utterance, and in all knowledge; Even as the testimony of Christ was confirmed in you.

2. **Romans 8:17** — And if children, then heirs; heirs of God, and joint-heirs with Christ.

3. **1 Corinthians 1:8,9** — Who shall also confirm you unto the end, that ye may be blameless in the day of our Lord Jesus Christ. God is faithful, by whom ye were called unto the fellowship of his Son Jesus Christ our Lord.

GREEK WORDS

1. "enriched" — **πλουτίζω** (*ploutidzo*): wealth so great it cannot be tabulated; abundant wealth; vast wealth; extreme riches; incredible abundance; magnificent opulence; extravagant lavishness; used by Plato to say no one was richer than legendary King Midas

2. "by" — **ἐν** (*en*): in or by

3. "joint-heirs" — **συγκληρονόμος** (*sunkleronomos*): a co-inheritor; a joint heir

4. "confirm" — **βεβαιόω** (*bebaioo*): authenticate, guarantee, or establish; make firm, sure, or steadfast; something proven to be true; a legal term used to validate that a document was trustworthy; if found trustworthy, it was established as authentic

5. "end" — **τέλος** (*telos*): conclusion; maturity

6. "fellowship" — **κοινωνία** (*koinonia*): fellowship; companionship; partnership

SYNOPSIS

Another marvelous cathedral in Saint Petersburg, Russia, is the Resurrection of Christ Church, which is also known as *the Church on Spilled Blood*. The history behind this cathedral dates back to 1881 when Alexander II was traveling by stagecoach to the Winter Palace, and while he was in route, a terrorist hurled a bomb under his carriage. The explosion badly damaged the wagon, killing three people and injuring several others.

Surprisingly, Alexander emerged from the carriage unharmed and immediately began to see if he could help those who had survived. When the terrorist saw him step out, he threw another bomb, which exploded just below Alexander's feet and blew off his legs. Rescuers quickly picked him up and rushed him into the Winter Palace. But within a few hours, Alexander II was pronounced dead.

His son, Alexander III, gave an order for a church to be built on the place where his father's blood had been spilled. Hence, the local people came to call it *the Church on Spilled Blood*. Today, the formal name of the cathedral is the Resurrection of Christ Church, and it is simply a remarkable place.

When people enter this cathedral, they are usually overwhelmed by its beauty, which is extravagantly displayed in numerous handcrafted mosaics. The fact is, there are more than 71,000 square feet of glistening mosaics in this church that tell the story of the life and ministry of Jesus. One particular mosaic depicts the outpouring of the Holy Spirit in the Upper Room on the Day of Pentecost. It marks the day that the Spirit of God began to empower men and women and equip us with supernatural gifts. It is these gifts of the Holy Spirit that bring the supernatural Jesus of the Bible to life!

The emphasis of this lesson:

As the gifts of the Holy Spirit are operating in and through our lives, we grow into a place of spiritual maturity and completeness. The gifts enable us to leave the mental realm and enter the experiential realm of knowing Jesus. Through the Person of the Holy Spirit, we join in a partnership with Christ, and His supernatural life becomes our real-life reality.

A REVIEW OF WHAT WE'VE LEARNED
The Grace of God Was Evident in Corinth

In First Corinthians 1:4, Paul wrote to the church in Corinth and said, "I thank my God always on your behalf, for the grace of God which is given you by Jesus Christ." We have seen that the word "grace" in this verse is the Greek word *charis*, and it was originally used to describe *a special touch conferred upon an individual or group of individuals by the gods*. Once *charis* — grace — was bestowed upon a person or group of people, it imparted to them superhuman abilities, enabling them to do what they could not normally or naturally do, and grace *always* came with outward evidence or visible demonstration.

In some Greek literature, the word *charis* (grace) was used to denote individuals who had been placed under a "magic spell" that transformed their personalities and imparted supernatural abilities to them. Hence, when the writers of the New Testament used the word "grace" (*charis*), it signified the supernatural touch of the One True God conferred upon individuals or a group of people, transforming and empowering them to be and do what they could not be or do before. This divine "favor" is not deserved and can't be earned. It is a manifestation of favor from God that is freely given.

Paul's words indicated that grace *always* comes with some *outward evidence* or *visible manifestation*, and in the case of the Corinthians, these visible manifestations included an abundance of the gifts of the Holy Spirit. When God poured out His grace on the believers in Corinth, He gave them supernatural abilities they previously did not have. They became spiritually rich because of the grace of God!

God's Grace Made Paul the Man He Was

Speaking of himself personally, Paul declared, "But by the grace of God I am what I am: and his grace which was bestowed upon me was not in vain; but I laboured more abundantly than they all: yet not I, but the grace of God which was with me" (1 Corinthians 15:10). Three times in this one verse, Paul pointed to the *grace* of God as being His source of divine strength and ability. Again, the word "grace" is the Greek word *charis*, which refers to that *supernatural touch of God that gives us the ability to be and do what we could never be and do on our own.*

Paul's words in First Corinthians 15:10 are the equivalent of him saying, "I am what I am because of the supernatural touch of God's grace on my life! His touch imparted to me abilities that I did not have. I would never be who I am today if God hadn't moved His grace into me and transformed me. As a result of His grace, I'm doing more than anyone else. The abilities I have are amazing, but it's not me. It's God's empowering grace that is partnering with me!"

Like Paul, when we cooperate with God's grace, it gives us supernatural abilities that are visible and never silent. When grace shows up in our lives or in our church, it comes with tangible, outward manifestations — just as it did in the lives of the believers in Corinth.

The Church of Corinth Was 'Enriched' With Spiritual Gifts

After recognizing that God's grace had been given to the believers in Corinth, Paul went on to say, "That in every thing ye are enriched by him, in all utterance, and in all knowledge" (1 Corinthians 1:5). We saw that the word "enriched" is a translation of the Greek word *ploutidzo*, which describes *wealth so great it cannot be tabulated*. It depicts *abundant wealth*; *vast wealth*; *extreme riches*; *incredible abundance*; *magnificent opulence*; or *extravagant lavishness*.

Furthermore, this word *ploutidzo* is where we get that word "plutocrat," which refers to *a person who is so rich that he is unable to ascertain the full extent of his own wealth*. This person's investments and companies — as well as the percentage of interest he earns on his portfolio — all grow so rapidly that his accountants and bookkeepers find it impossible to keep track of how much wealth he actually possesses. Interestingly, the word *ploutidzo* is the same word used by Plato to describe the riches of the legendary King Midas, whom he declared was the richest man to ever live up until that point.

Thus, the word *ploutidzo* — translated here as "enriched" — described someone who was "filthy stinking rich." And this is the word Paul used to describe the spiritual riches of the church in Corinth. When it came to spiritual gifts, the Corinthians were "filthy stinking rich"! The Spirit of God touched them, and they became spiritual plutocrats.

We, Too, Are Enriched — *In Him* and *By Him*

Paul wrote, "…In every thing ye are enriched by him…" (1 Corinthians 1:5). The word "by" in the Greek is the word *en*, and it can be translated as *in him* or *by him*. This tells us two important things: First, the day we were born again and placed *into Jesus Christ* was the richest day of our lives. It's the day we struck it rich!

If you are in Christ, you are one of God's children. "And if children, then heirs; heirs of God, and joint-heirs with Christ…" (Romans 8:17). In Greek, the word "joint-heirs" is a translation of the word *sunkleronomos*, which describes *a co-inheritor* or *a joint-heir*. This means on the day you got saved, you became a joint heir with Jesus Christ with a legal right to all the promises of God! Thus, First Corinthians 1:5 could be interpreted: "You were made rich the day you were placed *into* Him…."

Secondly, because the Greek word *en* can also be translated as *by him*, it emphasizes the point that this enrichment process isn't a one-time event — it is an *ongoing experience* that continues throughout our lives as long as we live in relationship with Christ. That said, we could interpret this part of the verse to say: "You are invested with great spiritual riches because you are in Him — and that's not all! The longer you remain in Him, you just keep getting blessed with more and more wealth that comes from being in Him."

In All 'Utterance' and in All 'Knowledge'

The apostle Paul went on to state that the believers in Corinth were enriched "…in all utterance, and in all knowledge" (1 Corinthians 1:5). Here we see Paul specifically pointing to the gifts of utterance and the gifts of knowledge that were operating powerfully in the Corinthian church.

The utterance — or *vocal gifts* — include tongues, interpretation of tongues, and prophecy. These are spiritual gifts that, when vocalized, supernaturally convey a message from the heart of God to a specific person or congregation. The knowledge — or *revelatory gifts* — include the word of wisdom, the word of knowledge, and discerning of spirits. These are spiritual gifts that supernaturally reveal the heart of God, the hearts of others, or facts and details that naturally could not be known.

It seems that the church in Corinth was *loaded* with the gifts of utterance and the gifts of knowledge. These gifts were in such great demonstration that Paul had to write an entire chapter about how to *manage* the huge overflow of these spiritual gifts in their gatherings (*see* 1 Corinthians 14).

What Do Spiritual Gifts Do For You and Your Church?

After declaring that the believers in Corinth were enriched with spiritual gifts, the apostle Paul went on to say, "Even as the testimony of Christ was confirmed in you" (1 Corinthians 1:6). Now you may be thinking, *What does he mean by "the testimony of Christ was confirmed in you"?* That's a good question.

Many Christians have a great deal of "head knowledge" concerning Jesus and the work of the Holy Spirit. They have read the Bible, studied books, and heard messages that have given them an overabundance of mental knowledge, but that is all they have. What they've read about they have not actually seen take place in the natural.

The fact is, until you actually see someone healed, the stories of Jesus healing people in the Gospels are just stories. Likewise, until you see a miracle manifest before your eyes, the accounts of Jesus working miracles are nothing more than words on a page. Just reading about an apostle moving in the gift of prophecy is not the same as hearing someone prophesy a future event and then seeing it take place. In other words, all the stories of Scripture remain in the intellectual realm until the gifts of the Holy Spirit begin to manifest. When the gifts of the Spirit work among us, "the testimony of Jesus" is confirmed.

When you see someone healed or miraculously restored before your very eyes, Christ is no longer just a historical Healer or Miracle Worker from the past. He is a present-day Healer and Miracle Worker! In this way, the gifts of healing and miracles give a personal "testimony" and confirm Christ as the Healer and Miracle Worker. The manifestation of each spiritual gift gives us practical experience with a facet of Jesus Christ in a way that supersedes mental knowledge.

The Gifts of the Spirit 'Confirm the Testimony of Jesus'

Just two verses later, the apostle Paul continues his message to the Corinthians by saying, "Who shall also confirm you unto the end, that ye may be blameless in the day of our Lord Jesus Christ" (1 Corinthians 1:8). The word "confirm" here is the Greek word *bebaioo*, which means *to authenticate, guarantee, establish; make firm, sure,* or *steadfast.* It depicts something proven to be true. It is a legal term used to validate that a document was trustworthy, and if it was found trustworthy, it was established as authentic.

When the gifts of the Holy Spirit are in operation, they "confirm" — validate, authenticate, and establish as trustworthy — the testimony of Jesus. Seeing the gifts in action causes what we believe about Jesus in the mental realm to enter the realm of reality and personal experience. The gifts of the Holy Spirit give us supernatural confirmation that God's Word is true and Jesus is who He says He is — He is *Healer, Prophet, Miracle Worker, Teacher,* and everything else the Bible claims Him to be.

Furthermore, the Scripture says these spiritual gifts confirm us unto the "end." The word "end" here is the Greek word *telos,* and it signifies a *conclusion,* which means the gifts of the Holy Spirit are to be in operation *until the conclusion* of the Church Age.

Equally important, the word *telos* also describes *maturity* or *perfection*, which means the gifts of the Spirit are intended to help us *grow in our faith* and become *spiritually complete*. They strengthen our faith and give us a solid understanding of who Jesus is. Thus, the idea that the gifts of the Holy Spirit cause a believer or congregation to become silly and carnal is just plain nonsense.

Jesus Becomes Our Spiritual Business Partner When the Gifts Are in Operation

In First Corinthians 1:9, Paul goes on to make this declaration: "God is faithful, by whom ye were called unto the fellowship of his Son Jesus Christ our Lord." The word "fellowship" in this verse is the Greek word *koinonia*, which describes *fellowship*, *companionship*, or *partnership*. It was the very word to depict a true, legitimate *business partner*. Paul used this word *koinonia* to describe how Jesus *partners* with us when the gifts of the Holy Spirit are in operation.

This word "fellowship" means when the gifts of the Holy Spirit are operating in the Church, they cause Jesus to supernaturally partner with you or with your church in a greater dimension. For example, a pastor can preach dynamically on the subject of healing, but when the gifts of healing actually manifest and people are supernaturally healed, the gift is the best message that *Jesus is a Healer!* Jesus literally becomes your partner by bringing His power and glory into the realm where you live.

In our next lesson, we'll continue our examination of why we need the gifts of the Holy Spirit.

STUDY QUESTIONS

Study to shew thyself approved unto God, a workman that needeth not to be ashamed, rightly dividing the word of truth.
— 2 Timothy 2:15

1. According to Mark 16:17 and 18, when you receive the power of the Spirit given by Jesus, what can you expect God to do through your life? (Also consider Luke 10:19; Matthew 18:18-20; Acts 1:8.)
2. Jesus operated in all the gifts of the Spirit, and as a result, He brought great glory to the Father. Look up these passages, and see if you can

identify the spiritual gift being demonstrated and what the results of the manifestation were.

- **The Woman at the Well** (John 4:16-19, 25-30, 39-42)
- **The Demon-Possessed Man of the Gadarenes** (Mark 5:1-14, 18-20)
- **Lazarus Raised from the Dead** (John 11:38-45)

PRACTICAL APPLICATION

But be ye doers of the word, and not hearers only, deceiving your own selves.
—James 1:22

1. What supernatural happenings — or gifts of the Spirit — have you witnessed with your own eyes?

2. How have these miraculous events made the Jesus of the Bible come alive in your life — validating and authenticating His Word is trustworthy?

3. The more yielded you become to the Holy Spirit, the more He can work through you to manifest His supernatural gifts. Take time now to pray and ask the Holy Spirit, *What changes do I need to make in the way I think, believe, and speak in order to see you move more consistently in and through my life?*

LESSON 5

TOPIC

Why We Need the Gifts of the Holy Spirit

SCRIPTURES

1. **1 Corinthians 1:4-6** — I thank my God always on your behalf, for the grace of God which is given you by Jesus Christ; That in every thing ye are enriched by him, in all utterance, and in all knowledge; Even as the testimony of Christ was confirmed in you.

2. **1 Corinthians 1:8,9** — Who shall also confirm you unto the end, that ye may be blameless in the day of our Lord Jesus Christ. God is faithful, by whom ye were called unto the fellowship of his Son Jesus Christ our Lord.

3. **Mark 16:20** — And they [the early preachers] went forth, and preached every where, the Lord working with them, and confirming the word with signs following. Amen.

4. **Hebrews 2:4** — God also bearing them witness, both with signs and wonders, and with divers miracles, and gifts of the Holy Ghost….

5. **1 Peter 4:10** — As every man hath received the gift, even so minister the same one to another, as good stewards of the manifold grace of God.

GREEK WORDS

1. "enriched" — πλουτίζω (*ploutidzo*): wealth so great it cannot be tabulated; abundant wealth; vast wealth; extreme riches; incredible abundance; magnificent opulence; extravagant lavishness; used by Plato to say no one was richer than legendary King Midas

2. "confirm" — βεβαιόω (*bebaioo*): authenticate, guarantee, or establish; make firm, sure, or steadfast; something proven to be true; a legal term used to validate that a document was trustworthy; if found trustworthy, it was established as authentic

3. "end" — τέλος (*telos*): conclusion; maturity

4. "fellowship" — κοινωνία (*koinonia*): fellowship; companionship; partnership

5. "working with them" — συνεργέω (*sunergeo*): from σύν (*sun*) and εργέω (*ergeo*); the word σύν (*sun*) denotes partnership; the word εργέω (*ergeo*) means to work; compounded, to work together, to participate together; depicts a joint partnership

6. "bearing them witness" — συνεπιμαρτυρέω (*sunepimartureo*): from σύν (*sun*) and μαρτύριον (*marturion*); the word σύν (*sun*) denotes partnership; the word μαρτύριον (*marturion*) denotes a testimony given in a court of law; working with someone else to present a legal case and to present undeniable evidence

7. "every man" — ἕκαστος (*hekastos*): every single person, no one excluded

SYNOPSIS

As we saw in the introduction of our previous lesson, the Resurrection of Christ Church in Saint Petersburg, Russia, is one of the most beautiful of all the cathedrals in the region. It was built to commemorate the life of Alexander II, who had been fatally wounded on the very ground where the church stands. It was officially consecrated in 1907 and is home to the largest exhibitions of mosaics in all of Europe.

More than 71,000 square feet of mosaics adorn this church, many of which depict the life and ministry of Jesus. There are portrayals of Jesus casting a demon out of a boy, Jesus walking on water, Jesus multiplying the loaves and fishes, Jesus healing the woman with the issue of blood, and so many other miracles Jesus did.

The Bible says, "…God anointed Jesus of Nazareth with the Holy Ghost and with power: who went about doing good, and healing all that were oppressed of the devil; for God was with him" (Acts 10:38). Clearly, the gifts of the Holy Spirit operated fully in Jesus. Every supernatural manifestation that took place in His life was a direct result of His partnership with the Holy Spirit. Jesus knew how to allow the gifts of the Spirit to flow through Him, which is what He wants us also to learn to do. When we partner with the Holy Spirit, it brings the miraculous presence of God into our lives and the lives of others.

The emphasis of this lesson:

Jesus Christ is alive *today*! And through the ministry of the Holy Spirit and the manifestation of His gifts, the supernatural reality of Jesus is brought to life right in front of us and into the midst of the Church. When the gifts of the Spirit manifest before our very eyes, the testimony of Jesus is authenticated and confirmed.

Facts or Fairy Tales:
How Do *You* View the Miracles of Jesus?

At the beginning of this teaching, Rick shared a story about one of his earliest visits to the State Hermitage Museum in Saint Petersburg, Russia, which is fabulous beyond description and deemed the most famous of all Russian museums. Initially, this building served as the Winter Palace of the Romanov family. Today, within its walls there is a huge collection of religious paintings that were assembled mostly from the time of Catherine the Great.

One room in the Hermitage is filled with an amazing assortment of paintings by Rembrandt. From a distance, one can make out that a number of these illustrations depict miraculous scenes from the life of Jesus. Once such portrait is a painting of Jesus raising Lazarus from the dead. The rich colors, the intricate details, and the moving images magnetically draw you in to take a closer look.

As Rick stood before this brilliant masterpiece, he noticed a small plaque on the base of the frame, which said "The Fairy Tale of Jesus Christ Raising Lazarus from the Dead." Stunned and shocked at the verbiage, he stepped away and began to take a closer look at several of the other Rembrandt paintings featuring miraculous scenes from the life of Christ. Amazingly, each description included the same tagline: "The Fairy Tales of Jesus Christ."

The purpose in calling the works of Jesus "fairy tales" was a communist attempt to put the Gospel on the same level as Peter Pan or Little Red Riding Hood. As offensive as this is, it certainly gives us reason to stop and think: Just how many professing *Christians* view the miraculous works of Jesus as mere fairy tales? Surprisingly, there are many devoted followers of Christ that sincerely love God, go to church every week, and read their Bibles who have relegated the miracles and healings of Jesus to a time in the past and to a group of people who no longer live.

The reason so many believers downplay the supernatural manifestations of Jesus and the apostles is because they have never personally witnessed Jesus' miracle-working power. Consequently, these Christians can only fantasize and try to imagine what Jesus' miracles must have been like. Virtually everything they know about Jesus is purely mental, imaginary, or speculative — similar to the way one would view a hero in a fairy tale. But God never intended for Jesus to be only a historical figure who did something in the past. The fact is, Jesus is alive *today*! And through the ministry of the Holy Spirit — and His gifts — the supernatural reality of Jesus is brought to life right in front of us and into the midst of the Church!

Make no mistake! "Jesus Christ [is] the same yesterday, and to day, and for ever" (Hebrews 13:8). What He did *then* is what He is still doing *now* and will continue doing in the future. The way He accomplishes His work today is through the power of the Holy Spirit living, breathing, and working through you and the Body of Christ.

Spiritually Speaking, We Are 'Filthy Stinking Rich'

As Paul began his first letter to the church in Corinth, he said, "I thank my God always on your behalf, for the grace of God which is given you by Jesus Christ; that in every thing ye are enriched by him, in all utterance, and in all knowledge" (1 Corinthians 1:4,5). We have seen that the word "enriched" is the Greek word *ploutidzo*, and it describes *wealth so great it cannot be tabulated.* It denotes *abundant wealth; vast wealth; extreme riches; incredible abundance; magnificent opulence;* or *extravagant lavishness.*

This word *ploutidzo* is the very same word used by Plato to describe the legendary King Midas who was said to be the richest man in the world at that time. It's also the word where we get the word "plutocrat," which refers to *a person who is so rich that he is unable to ascertain the full extent of his own wealth.* This person's investments and companies — as well as the percentage of interest he earns on his portfolio — all keep growing so rapidly that his accountants and bookkeepers find it impossible to keep track of how much wealth he actually possesses.

Amazingly, this word *ploutidzo* — translated here as "enriched" — is the word the Holy Spirit prompted Paul to use to describe what happens when the grace of God is poured into us. Spiritually speaking, it makes us "filthy stinking rich"! This is what the church in Corinth was experiencing, and it came particularly in the form of the gifts of the Holy Spirit. When the Spirit of God touched them, they became *spiritual plutocrats.*

The Church in Corinth Was Loaded With Vocal and Revelatory Gifts

Paul said the specific kinds of riches that were thriving in the church in Corinth were gifts of "utterance" and gifts of "knowledge." Utterance — or *vocal gifts* — include *tongues, interpretation of tongues,* and *prophecy.* These are spiritual gifts that, when vocalized, supernaturally convey a message from the heart of God to a specific person or congregation.

There were also many knowledge gifts on display in Corinth. Also referred to as *revelatory gifts,* these include the *word of wisdom,* the *word of knowledge*, and *discerning of spirits*. These are spiritual gifts that supernaturally convey and reveal the heart of God, the hearts of others, or facts and details that naturally could not be known.

What's interesting is that the church in Corinth was so *rich* in these kinds of spiritual gifts that Paul had to take time to write an entire chapter with instructions on how to *manage* the mighty overflow of these gifts in their gatherings (*see* 1 Corinthians 14). Sadly, while most churches today are praying and longing for the gifts of the Spirit to manifest, the church in Corinth had to learn how to manage the multiple demonstrations of these spiritual gifts in order to avoid confusion and maintain order.

Seeing the Gifts of the Spirit in Action Is the Game-Changer

Paul told the believers in Corinth that they were enriched with spiritual gifts, "Even as the testimony of Christ was confirmed in you" (1 Corinthians 1:6). The word "testimony" here describes who Jesus is. In other words, the "testimony of Christ" is that He is Healer, Miracle Worker, Prophet, Teacher, and One who does the impossible. That is what we read about in God's Word. But if all we ever do is read about the supernatural side of Jesus and never see it in action, our understanding of who Jesus is extremely limited.

The truth is, many Christians have heard a great deal about Jesus and the work of the Holy Spirit. They have acquired much head knowledge from reading the Bible, studying books, and listening to messages. Unfortunately, a great number of these believers have also been taught that the miracles of Jesus and the gifts of the Holy Spirit ceased with the death of the apostles. Therefore, for them, the supernatural manifestations of Scripture remain confined to the mental realm. Maybe this is something you yourself have experienced.

The fact is, until you actually see someone healed, the stories of Jesus healing people in the Gospels are like fairy tales. Likewise, until you see a miracle manifest before your eyes, the reports of Jesus working miracles are nothing more than words on a page. Just reading about Jesus knowing the thoughts of the Pharisees (*see* Luke 5:21-26) or reciting the life history of the Samaritan woman (*see* John 4:16-19) is not the same as seeing someone move in these gifts right in front of you.

However, when the gifts of the Holy Spirit begin to manifest before your very eyes, "the testimony of Jesus" is confirmed. When you see someone who is confined to a wheelchair get up and walk, the Jesus of the Bible comes alive. When you personally witness a blind person receive their sight or a deaf person begin hearing, Christ is no longer just a historical Healer or Miracle Worker from the past. He is a present-day Healer and Miracle Worker!

In this way, the gifts of healing and miracles give a personal "testimony" and confirm Christ as the Healer and Miracle Worker. The manifestation of each spiritual gift gives us practical experience with a facet of Jesus Christ in a way that supersedes mental knowledge. The demonstration of the gifts of the Spirit takes what we know about Jesus out of the mental, imaginary realm and brings it into the realm of reality.

The Operation of the Gifts Authenticate Who Jesus Is

The apostle Paul went on to say that the Lord Himself would "...confirm you unto the end, that ye may be blameless in the day of our Lord Jesus Christ" (1 Corinthians 1:8). The word "confirm" here is the Greek word *bebaioo*, which means *to authenticate, guarantee, establish; make firm, sure,* or *steadfast.* It depicts *something proven to be true.* It was a legal term used to validate that a document was trustworthy, and if it was found trustworthy, it was established as authentic.

The use of the word *bebaioo* — translated here as "confirm" — tells us that when the gifts of the Spirit are in operation, they validate, authenticate, and establish as trustworthy the testimony of Jesus. The gifts of the Holy Spirit give us supernatural confirmation that God's Word is true and Jesus is who He says He is— He is *Healer, Prophet, Miracle Worker, Teacher,* and everything else the Bible claims Him to be.

What's more, the Bible says when the gifts of the Spirit manifest, they "...confirm you unto the end..." (1 Corinthians 1:8). The word "end" here is the Greek word *telos*, and it indicates a *conclusion*, which means the gifts of the Holy Spirit are to be in operation *until the conclusion* of the Church age.

But that is not the only meaning of the word *telos.* It is also used to describe *maturity* or *completion.* This means the gifts of the Spirit are intended to help us grow and become *spiritually mature* in our faith. They strengthen us and give us a solid, experiential understanding of who Jesus is. The supernatural element of His life is no longer something we just mentally agree to. Rather, we know it to be real by personal experience.

We Are Called Into Partnership With Jesus

In First Corinthians 1:9, Paul went on to say, "God is faithful, by whom ye were called unto the fellowship of his Son Jesus Christ our Lord." In Greek, the word for "fellowship" is *koinonia*, which describes *fellowship*, *companionship*, or *partnership*. It was the very word to depict a true, legitimate *business partner*. Paul's use of this word *koinonia* tells us that when the gifts of the Holy Spirit are in operation, it brings us into *partnership* with Jesus.

This portrait of a divine partnership between Jesus and the Church can be clearly seen in Mark 16:20, which says, "And they [the early preachers] went forth, and preached every where, **the Lord working with them**, and confirming the word with signs following." The phrase "working with them" is a translation of the Greek word *sunergeo*, which is a compound of the words *sun* and *ergeo*. The word *sun* denotes *partnership*, and the word *ergeo* means *to work*. When these words are compounded, it means *to work together* or *to participate together*. It is the picture of a joint partnership.

What happens when we actively join in partnership with Jesus? The Bible says we go about "…confirming the word with signs following" (Mark 16:20). The word "confirming" here is again the Greek word *bebaioo*, which means *to authenticate*, *guarantee*, *establish*; or *make sure*. This tells us that through our partnering with Jesus, the Holy Spirit authenticates that our message is trustworthy through the manifestation of the spiritual gifts.

We see this principle confirmed in Hebrews 2:4, where the writer says, "God also bearing them witness, both with signs and wonders, and with divers miracles, and gifts of the Holy Ghost." The phrase "bearing them witness" is a translation of the Greek word *sunepimartureo*, which is a compound of the words *sun* and *marturion*. The word *sun* denotes *partnership*, and the word *marturion*, denotes *a testimony given in a court of law*. When these words are joined together, it depicts *working with someone else to present a legal case and to present undeniable evidence*.

Once again we see God partnering with those who proclaim the Gospel message. When the gifts of the Holy Spirit operate in conjunction with the preaching of the Gospel, those gifts provide *tangible demonstrations* of

Jesus Christ. It's true that these believers could have preached the Gospel without supernatural signs and wonders, and the message would still have been true. However, the manifestation of the spiritual gifts gave strength to the message — validating and proving that it was indeed from Heaven.

Friend, just as early believers partnered with Jesus on this supernatural level, we too must partner with Him by cooperating with the gifts of the Holy Spirit. In our next lesson, we will dive into the examination of the first five gifts of the Holy Spirit: the *word of wisdom*, the *word of knowledge*, the gift of *faith*, the *gifts of healing*, and the *working of miracles*.

STUDY QUESTIONS

Study to shew thyself approved unto God, a workman that needeth not to be ashamed, rightly dividing the word of truth.
— 2 Timothy 2:15

1. Stop and think: What would the message of the gospel be like had there never been any supernatural signs and wonders accompanying it? If Jesus and the apostles had never performed miracles, how do you think people would have received Jesus' message both then and now? How would your perception and reception of the Gospel change?

2. Having a personal, firsthand experience with Jesus through the Holy Spirit is very important. Take a few moments to carefully meditate on this portion of Paul's prayer for the Ephesian believers and for *all believers* in all generations.

   "May He grant you out of the rich treasury of His glory to be strengthened and reinforced with mighty power in the inner man by the [Holy] Spirit [Himself indwelling your innermost being and personality]. [That you may really come] to know [practically, through experience for yourselves] the love of Christ, which far surpasses mere knowledge [without experience]; that you may be filled [through all your being] unto all the fullness of God [may have the richest measure of the divine Presence, and become a body wholly filled and flooded with God Himself]!"
   — Ephesians 3:16,19 (*AMPC*)

   What is the Holy Spirit speaking to you in these verses about having personal experiences with Him?

PRACTICAL APPLICATION

**But be ye doers of the word, and not hearers only,
deceiving your own selves.
— James 1:22**

1. When you hear and read about the miraculous works of Jesus and the apostles, how do you view them? As mere fairy tales or actual events that displayed the power of God?

2. Is what you know about Jesus purely mental, imaginary, and speculative? Or have you personally seen and witnessed the supernatural demonstration of His power?

3. If you have seen the gifts of the Holy Spirit manifested, how have they given you supernatural confirmation that God's Word is true and Jesus is who He says He is? In what ways have you personally witnessed Jesus as your *Healer, Prophet, Miracle Worker, Teacher*, etc.?

LESSON 6

TOPIC

The Gifts of the Holy Spirit, Part 1

SCRIPTURES

1. **1 Corinthians 12:7** — But the manifestation of the Spirit is given to every man to profit withal.

2. **1 Corinthians 12:4-6** — Now there are diversities of gifts, but the same Spirit. And there are differences of administrations, but the same Lord. And there are diversities of operations, but it is the same God which worketh all in all.

3. **1 Corinthians 12:8-10** — For to one is given by the Spirit the word of wisdom; to another the word of knowledge by the same Spirit; To another faith by the same Spirit; to another the gifts of healing by the same Spirit; To another the working of miracles; to another prophecy; to another discerning of spirits; to another divers kinds of tongues; to another the interpretation of tongues.

4. **Romans 12:3** — …God hath dealt to every man the measure of faith.

GREEK WORDS

1. "manifestation" — **φανέρωσις** (*phanerosis*): apparent; appear; manifest; visible; something that is seen; conspicuous; observable; obvious; clear; open; apparent or evident

2. "every man" — **ἔκαστος** (*hekastos*): an all-inclusive term that embraces everyone, with no one excluded

3. "profit" — **συμφέρω** (*sumphero*): a joint or shared benefit; always profitable

4. "gifts" — **χάρισμα** (*charisma*): from **χάρις** (*charis*), the word for grace; here it is a form of **χάρισμα** (*charisma*), which is a grace-imparted enablement

5. "administration" — **διακονία** (*diakonia*): ministries; ways of serving; what they bring to the table

6. "operations" — **ἐνέργημα** (*energema*): effects; outcomes; results

7. "word" — **λόγος** (*logos*): a word; not a whole message, but a fragmentary word

8. "wisdom" — **σοφία** (*sophia*): insight; special insight not naturally known

9. "word of wisdom" — a fragment of special insight not naturally known

10. "word" — **λόγος** (*logos*): a word; not a whole message, but a fragmentary word

11. "knowledge" — **γνῶσις** (*gnosis*): knowledge

12. "word of knowledge" — a fragment of special knowledge not naturally known

13. "faith" — **πίστις** (*pistis*): faith; belief

14. "gifts" — **χαρίσματα** (*charismata*): from **χάρισμα** (*charisma*) from **χάρις** (*charis*), the word for grace; here it is the plural form for grace-imparted enablements

15. "healing" — **ἰάομαι** (*iaomai*): to cure; to be doctored; a healing power that progressively reverses a condition; mostly denotes a healing that comes to pass over a period of time; often translated as a treatment or cure or remedy; depicts a sickness that is progressively rather than instantaneously healed

16. "working of miracles" — **ἐνεργήματα δυνάμεων** (*energemata dunameon*): **ἐνεργέω** (*energeo*) and **δύναμις** (*dunamis*); the word

ἐνεργέω (*energeo*) pictures energy; the word δύναμις (*dunamis*) speaks of power or a force of nature like a hurricane, tornado, earthquake, or the full, advancing force of an army; as ἐνεργήματα δυνάμεων (*energemata dunameon*), depicts an energizing of terrific power that is beyond human ability to perform; miraculous power or miraculous manifestations

SYNOPSIS

In 1930, approximately 23 years after the Resurrection of Christ Church was consecrated and opened, the communist regime took over and closed its doors. What was once a center of worship was turned into a warehouse for storing potatoes. The new Marxist leaders' plan was to totally demolish the church, so they began their work by removing the church's bells and melting them down to repurpose the metal for something else. But before they could go any further, the events of WWII interrupted their efforts, and they decided to turn the church into a morgue.

Once the war was over, Resurrection of Christ Church went back to being a warehouse — only this time it was used to store props from a local theater in Saint Petersburg. Eventually, in the late 1960s, a decision was made to renovate the building and reopen it as a museum. For the next 27 years, teams of people worked tirelessly to refresh, renew, and rebuild this church. The restoration process was very long and required a great deal of manpower and management. In fact, it took three years longer to renovate the church than it did to initially build it. Nevertheless, in 1997, Resurrection of Christ Church reopened its doors as a museum, and today it functions once again as a church.

In a similar way, there are many churches today that have fallen into major disrepair spiritually. Some seem more like museums that house relics of the past, while others are more like morgues because there is no life left in them. The reason for this is that these churches are no longer making room for the Holy Spirit to move and manifest His gifts. To breathe life back into these churches and put them in proper working order, the gifts of the Holy Spirit must be reinstated and embraced in the church. It will take time, but with dedication, determination, and obedience to the leading of the Spirit, new life will return, and the Spirit will once again begin manifesting His gifts.

The emphasis of this lesson:

There are many kinds of spiritual gifts, and each one of them brings something unique to the Body of Christ that produces a much needed outcome. The first five gifts of the Holy Spirit are the word of wisdom, the word of knowledge, faith, gifts of healing, and the working of miracles.

The Manifestations of the Spirit
Are for Every Single Believer

In First Corinthians 12, the apostle Paul begins talking about the gifts of the Holy Spirit, and in verse 7 he says, "But the manifestation of the Spirit is given to every man to profit withal." Notice the word "manifestation." In Greek, it is the word *phanerosis*, and it means *to appear* or *manifest*. It describes *something apparent, visible,* or *something that is seen*. It indicates *something conspicuous, observable, obvious, clear, open,* or *evident*. This tells us that when the gifts of the Holy Spirit begin to operate, the presence of the Spirit becomes very visible, clear, and obvious in our midst.

Also notice the Scripture says that the manifestation of the Spirit is given to "every man." In Greek, the words "every man" are a translation of the word *hekastos*, which is an all-inclusive term that embraces *everyone, with no one excluded*. The Spirit's manifestation is given to every believer and is for every believer's "profit." The word "profit" is the Greek word *sumphero*, and it describes *a joint or shared benefit; something that is always profitable*. Thus, spiritual gifts benefit the entire Church and give believers a supernatural advantage.

Now you know why the devil is against the manifestation of the gifts of the Spirit. He knows that these spiritual gifts are beneficial and instrumental in giving believers the advantage over him. This is why Satan has withstood their operation in the Church and even tried to theologically convince people that the gifts of the Spirit passed away with the death of the apostles. The devil knows that when the supernatural element of the Holy Spirit is evident and at work in the Church, it brings a dimension of Christ to the Church that believers otherwise do not know.

There Are Multiple Types
of 'Gifts, Administrations, and Operations'

Let's back up a few verses and take a look at what the apostle Paul stated as he first began to talk about the gifts of the Spirit. In First Corinthians 12:4, he wrote, "Now there are diversities of gifts, but the same Spirit." The word "gifts" here is the Greek word *charisma*, which is taken from the word *charis*, the word for *grace*. In this verse, it's a form of *charisma*, which is a *grace-imparted enablement*, and because it's plural, it means there are *multiple* kinds of spiritual manifestations.

In First Corinthians 12:5, Paul added, "And there are differences of administrations, but the same Lord." The word "administrations" is the Greek word *diakonia*, and it describes *ministries* or *ways of serving*. Basically, this describes what is being *brought to the table*. Each spiritual gift brings something unique to the table that each member of the Church benefits from.

In the very next verse, Paul said, "And there are diversities of operations, but it is the same God which worketh all in all" (1 Corinthians 12:6). Here we see the use of the word "operations," which is a translation of the Greek word *energema*, and it describes *effects*, *outcomes*, or *results*.

So in these three verses, we see there are multiple kinds of spiritual gifts or manifestations of God's grace, and every one of them brings something unique and special to the table. And because they each bring something special to the Church, they each produce different — much needed — results or outcomes.

THE FIRST FIVE GIFTS
The Word of Wisdom

The apostle Paul continues his teaching on the gifts of the Holy Spirit in First Corinthians 12:8, saying, "For to one is given by the Spirit the word of wisdom...." Here we see the word "word," which is the Greek term *logos*, and it describes *a word*. It is not a whole message, but *a fragmentary message*. The word "wisdom" in Greek is *sophia*, which describes *insight* or *special insight not naturally known*. When these words are joined to form the phrase "word of wisdom," it describes *a fragment of special insight not naturally known*.

This gift of the Holy Spirit operates in a moment when a fragment of special insight is supernaturally revealed to an individual about a specific situation. It's received as wisdom because it delivers an answer or a directive to a pressing need to a question or situation. A "word of wisdom" can also provide insight into future events that could not naturally be known.

An example of this gift is found in Acts 27:24 when the apostle Paul was on a ship with others and they were heading for disaster. After the crew's long struggle to bring the ship under control, God gave Paul a "word of wisdom" through a dream, "Saying, Fear not, Paul; thou must be brought before Caesar: and, lo, God hath given thee all that sail with thee."

Please note this "word of wisdom" did not give Paul all the answers regarding his situation. It was a fragmentary word from Heaven for that pressing moment that gave direction and insight into the future for his situation. He supernaturally received a partial word, letting him know they would survive because he was destined to stand before Caesar in Rome and testify about Jesus.

The Word of Knowledge

In addition to the "word of wisdom," Paul included a second gift of the Spirit in First Corinthians 12:8, which is called the "word of knowledge." Again, we see the word "word," which is the Greek term *logos*, and it describes not a whole message, but *a fragmentary message*. The word "knowledge" is the Greek word *gnosis*, which means *knowledge*. When these words are joined to form the phrase "word of knowledge," it describes *a fragment of special knowledge not naturally known*.

Basically, the "word of knowledge" is the ability to supernaturally know facts and details that one could never know naturally. When a "word of knowledge" is given to a believer by the Holy Spirit, it is often imparted to illuminate listeners to God's intimate, personal involvement in the facts and details of a specific situation or of a person's life so that His purpose can be fulfilled in that situation or in that individual's life.

An example of a "word of knowledge" is found in John 4:5-30 when Jesus was at the well in Samaria and he met a woman who came to draw water. As Jesus talked with her, certain facts and details about her life were instantly and supernaturally revealed to Him. Although Jesus was not given every detail about the Samaritan woman, the Holy Spirit did reveal a significant amount of her personal information to Him that immediately made her aware of His tender care and involvement in her life.

The Gift of Faith

The third gift of the Holy Spirit is found in First Corinthians 12:9, which says, "To another faith by the same Spirit…." In Greek, the word "faith" is *pistis*, which is the word for *faith* or *belief*. It is important to note that the "gift of faith" is different from the personal "measure of faith" that God gives to every single person (*see* Romans 12:3).

The "gift of faith" Paul talks about in First Corinthians 12:9 is a special faith that manifests as a sudden impartation of the Holy Spirit. It is a supernatural ability to believe for God to accomplish His purpose of desire in a particular situation or event. When this supernatural burst of faith is suddenly released in a believer by the Spirit, that believer is empowered to believe the impossible is doable in order to accomplish what can only be done supernaturally.

An example of the "gift of faith" is found in Acts 14:8 and 9, where Paul was preaching to a group of pagans in Lystra and he suddenly sensed a burst of special faith in a lame man to be healed. In that moment, the Bible says, "[Paul] said with a loud voice, Stand upright on thy feet. And he leaped and walked" (Acts 14:10). When Paul recognized the divine "gift of faith," he acted on it, and as a result, the impossible became a reality!

The Gifts of Healing

Immediately after mentioning the gift of faith, Paul reveals the next gift of the Spirit, which the Bible calls the "gifts of healing" (1 Corinthians 12:9). Interestingly, the word "gifts" is plural. Again, just as in First Corinthians 12:8, the word "gifts" is taken from the Greek word *charis* the word for *grace*. Here, it is the Greek word *charisma*, the plural form for *grace*, meaning *imparted enablements*. The fact that "gifts" is plural lets us know that there are multiple ways God produces healing.

The Greek word for "healing" in this verse is *iaomai*, which is a very important word. It is an old term that means *to cure* or *to be doctored*, which means it can refer to healing that takes place through the work of a medical doctor. This word *iaomai* depicts *a healing power that progressively reverses a condition* and mostly denotes a healing that comes to pass over a period of time. Oftentimes, it is translated as the word *treatment, cure* or *remedy*, and it depicts a sickness that is progressively healed rather than instantaneously healed.

Very often, the "gifts of healing" are a manifestation of the Holy Spirit that begins with a prayer or with believers laying hands on the one who is sick and praying for him or her. At that point, the healing (*iaomai*) is initiated, but it will fully come into effect over a period of time. Although this healing is divine in nature, this gift of the Spirit refers to progressive results rather than instantaneous results.

An example of the "gifts of healing" in operation is seen in Luke 17 when Jesus met a group of lepers who needed His healing touch. "And when he saw them, he said unto them, Go shew yourselves unto the priests. And it came to pass, that, as they went, they were cleansed" (Luke 17:14). This supernatural touch of the Holy Spirit working through Jesus took place progressively *as they went.*

The Working of Miracles

The fifth gift of the Holy Spirit is revealed in First Corinthians 12:10, and it is called the "working of miracles." The phrase "working of miracles" in Greek is *energemata dunameon*, which is taken from the words *energeo* and *dunamis*. The word *energeo* pictures *energy*, and the word *dunamis* speaks of *power* or a force of nature like a hurricane, tornado, or an earthquake; it can also denote the full, advancing force of an army. When these two words come together in the form of *energemata dunameon* — translated here as "working of miracles" — it depicts *an energizing of terrific power that is beyond human ability to perform; miraculous power or miraculous manifestations.*

What's interesting is that in the original Greek text of First Corinthians 12:10, the phrase "working of miracles" actually appears as the "operation of powers." Hence, when Paul wrote these words, he was describing a divine operation of supernatural power that overrides natural laws and immediately does what is not naturally possible.

With regards to the human body, the "working of miracles" is displayed when a damaged organ or limb is instantly and supernaturally healed and restored. God's power suddenly manifests, speeding up a healing process that would normally take place over a long period of time or that would perhaps never naturally occur. In the blink of an eye, the process is miraculously completed.

Another example of the "working of miracles" would be a supernatural overriding of the laws of nature that enable one to do what no human could naturally do. For instance, when Jesus walked on the water, it was a "working of miracles." Likewise, when He multiplied the loaves and fish to feed thousands of people, it was a "working of miracles." In that critical moment, the power of God showed up and supernaturally transformed and multiplied the food Jesus held in His hands. Although this instantaneous multiplication of physical matter is impossible in the natural, the power of God overrode the laws of nature and made the impossible become possible — and God got the glory!

In our next lesson, we will continue our study and learn about the remaining four gifts of the Holy Spirit Paul listed in First Corinthians 12. These include *prophecy*, *discerning of spirits*, *divers kinds of tongues*, and *interpretation of tongues*.

STUDY QUESTIONS

> **Study to shew thyself approved unto God, a workman that needeth not to be ashamed, rightly dividing the word of truth.**
> **— 2 Timothy 2:15**

1. According to James 3:17, how can you know for certain that the knowledge and wisdom you are hearing from someone is truly from Heaven?

2. Take a moment to reflect on the meaning of the "gifts of healing" and the "working of miracles," and in your own words, briefly explain the difference between the two. Have you been the recipient of either of these gifts? If so, which one? What took place?

3. If there was anything that touched Jesus' heart and moved Him to action, it was great faith. What was the element of great faith demonstrated by each of these individuals?
   - **The Centurion** (Matthew 8:5-13)
   - **The Canaanite Woman** (Matthew 15:22-28)
   - **The Afflicted Woman** (Mark 5:25-34)

PRACTICAL APPLICATION

**But be ye doers of the word, and not hearers only,
deceiving your own selves.
— James 1:22**

1. What do you think scares Satan most about the gifts of the Holy Spirit operating in your life and in your church?

2. The Bible says, "Each person is given something to do that shows who God is: Everyone gets in on it, everyone benefits" (1 Corinthians 12:7 *MSG*). What fellow believers come to mind that you are truly grateful for their gifting? What spiritual gifts do they bring to the table that show who God is? How do you benefit from their gift — how do they bless your life?

3. Has someone ever given you a *word of wisdom* or a *word of knowledge* from God that was spot-on accurate? What was the word? How did it confirm what God was already speaking to you in your personal time with Him? How did the manifestation of this gift affect your faith?

LESSON 7

TOPIC

The Gifts of the Holy Spirit, Part 2

SCRIPTURES

1. **1 Corinthians 12:4-7** — Now there are diversities of gifts, but the same Spirit. And there are differences of administrations, but the same Lord. And there are diversities of operations, but it is the same God which worketh all in all. But the manifestation of the Spirit is given to every man to profit withal.

2. **1 Corinthians 12:10** — To another the working of miracles; to another prophecy; to another discerning of spirits; to another divers kinds of tongues; to another the interpretation of tongues.

3. **1 Corinthians 14:3** — But he that prophesieth speaketh unto men to edification, and exhortation, and comfort.

4. **Matthew 9:4** — And Jesus knowing their thoughts said, Wherefore think ye evil in your hearts?

GREEK WORDS

1. "gifts" — χάρισμα (*charisma*): from χάρις (*charis*), the word for grace; here it is a form of χάρισμα (*charisma*), which is a grace-imparted enablement
2. "administration" — διακονία (*diakonia*): ministries; ways of serving; what they bring to the table
3. "operations" — ἐνέργημα (*energema*): effects; outcomes; results
4. "manifestation" — φανέρωσις (*phanerosis*): apparent; appear; manifest; visible; something that is seen; conspicuous; observable; obvious; clear; open; apparent or evident
5. "every man" — ἕκαστος (*hekastos*): an all-inclusive term that embraces everyone, with no one excluded
6. "profit" — συμφέρω (*sumphero*): a joint or shared benefit; always profitable
7. "prophecy" — προφητεία (*propheteia*): a compound of the words πρό (*pro*) and φημί (*phemi*); the word πρό (*pro*) is used in connection with *phemi*, which always means to say or to speak; the word *phemi* lets us know this is a speaking or saying gift; pictures one who supernaturally speaks on behalf of God, in advance of a situation, to foretell an event or to assert the mind of God to others
8. "discerning" — διάκρισις (*diakrisis*): distinguishing; perceiving; discerning
9. "spirits" — πνευμάτων (*pneumaton*): plural, spirits or spiritual situations
10. "discerning of spirits" — διακρίσεις πνευμάτων (*diakriseis pneumaton*): perceiving things that are spiritual
11. "tongues" — γλῶσσα (*glossa*): tongues, languages; glossolalia
12. "interpretation" — ἑρμηνεία (*hermeneia*): an interpretation; giving the gist of a message rather than a translation; an equivalent meaning and not a word-for-word rendering

SYNOPSIS

In the city of Saint Petersburg, Russia, there stands another magnificent towering cathedral — the Cathedral of Peter and Paul. It's the first and oldest landmark in Saint Petersburg and was built under the direction of Peter the Great between 1712 and 1733 near the Neva River. It boasts of one of the tallest church bell towers in the world, and it is truly a place of marvelous workmanship that is both elaborate and intricate.

When the communist regime took over, preserving the imperial history was abandoned, and the Cathedral of Peter and Paul fell into terrible disrepair. Many decades passed, and the care and upkeep were eventually entrusted into the hands of new management who painstakingly restored the cathedral's original beauty. Once again its magnificent interiors of precious stones, precious metals, and more than 22 pounds of gold glisten with splendor.

As a believer, you are the temple of the Holy Spirit (*see* 1 Corinthians 6:19) — a cathedral for His magnificent presence. He has embellished you with the riches of the name of Jesus, the blood of Jesus, the Word of God, and the gifts of the Spirit. The question is, how are you managing the riches He has entrusted to you? If your temple has fallen into disrepair, today is a great day to begin managing things better.

The emphasis of this lesson:

The gifts of the Holy Spirit are for everyone and are instrumental in giving believers an advantage over Satan. Prophecy, discerning of spirits, tongues, and interpretation of tongues are also power manifestations of the Spirit to direct, encourage, strengthen, and reveal truth to us as believers.

The Gifts of the Spirit Are for Everyone and Make God's Presence Evident

In First Corinthians 12, the apostle Paul unveils nine specific gifts of the Holy Spirit and explains how they're to function in the Church. Who are these gifts for? First Corinthians 12:7 says, "But the manifestation of the Spirit is given to every man to profit withal." Here we see the word "manifestation," which is the Greek word *phanerosis*, and it means *to appear* or *manifest*. It describes *something apparent, visible,* or *something that is seen.* It indicates *something conspicuous, observable, obvious, clear, open,* or *evident.* This lets us know that when the gifts of the Holy Spirit are in operation, we can clearly and tangibly see the Spirit's presence in our midst.

These gifts are directly from the Holy Spirit, so there is no need to be afraid of them. He only gives us what is good. And they are "given" — the Greek word *didomi*, which means *imparted* or *offered* — to "every man." In Greek, the words "every man" are a translation of the word *hekastos*, which is an all-inclusive term that embraces *everyone, with no one excluded.* Thus, the gifts of the Spirit are not given just to a select few in a certain denomination. If you are born again, God wants you to have them. These manifestations are given to every believer and are for everyone's "profit." The word "profit" is the Greek word *sumphero*, and it describes *a joint or shared benefit; something that is always profitable.* When the gifts are operating, all believers experience some kind of supernatural advantage.

This is why the devil fights against the demonstration of the gifts of the Spirit. He knows that these supernatural manifestations bring the living presence of Jesus right into the Church, causing us to move from the mental realm of knowing Jesus to the experiential realm of knowing Him. Indeed, the gifts of the Spirit are instrumental in giving believers the advantage over Satan.

The Array of Gifts Produces an Array of Results

Looking again at First Corinthians 12:4, the apostle Paul said, "Now there are diversities of gifts, but the same Spirit." We learned that the word "gifts" is the Greek word *charisma*, which is taken from the word *charis*, the word for *grace*. Here, it's a form of *charisma*, which describes a *grace-imparted enablement*, and because it's plural, it means there are multiple kinds of spiritual manifestations.

Paul went on to say, "And there are differences of administrations, but the same Lord" (1 Corinthians 12:5). The word "administrations" is the Greek word *diakonia*, and it describes *various ministries* or *ways of serving*. It is the picture of a servant who serves someone at a table. This lets us know that each spiritual gift brings something unique to the table that the Church benefits from.

In addition to the diversities of gifts and differences of administrations, Paul said, "And there are diversities of operations, but it is the same God which worketh all in all" (1 Corinthians 12:6). Here we see the use of the word "operations," which is a translation of the Greek word *energema*, and it describes *effects, outcomes,* or *results*. This word indicates that each of the gifts ultimately produce a unique and specific outcome in each of our lives.

So in these three verses, we see that there are multiple kinds of spiritual gifts or manifestations of God's grace, and each of them brings something unique to the table. And because they each bring something special to the Church, they each produce diverse — but much needed — results or outcomes.

The first five gifts of the Spirit that we examined in our previous lesson are the *word of wisdom, the word of knowledge*, the *gift of faith*, the *gifts of healing*, and the *working of miracles*, which in the Greek is actually rendered as the *operation of divine powers*. This describes situations when the power of God is released and it overrides natural laws, instantaneously accomplishing what normally would take a long period of time to occur or that would perhaps never naturally occur at all.

THE REMAINING FOUR GIFTS OF THE SPIRIT
The Gift of Prophecy

In First Corinthians 12:10, the apostle Paul lists five gifts of the Spirit. Just after mentioning the *working of miracles*, he adds the sixth gift, which is *prophecy*. In Greek, the word "prophecy" is *propheteia*, which is a compound of the words *pro* and *phemi*. The word *pro* means *in front of* or *before*, and the word *phemi* always means *to say* or *to speak*, which lets us know this is a speaking or saying gift. When *pro* and *phemi* are compounded to form the word *prophecy*, it pictures *one who supernaturally speaks on behalf of God* or *to speak in advance of a situation*. It can also mean *to foretell an event* or *to assert the mind of God to others*.

It's important to note that one who speaks a prophetic word to the Church is not necessarily called into the fulltime ministry of a prophet. In First Corinthians 14:1, Paul — under the inspiration of the Holy Spirit — encouraged all believers to seek the gift of prophecy along with all the other gifts. Therefore, everyone can prophesy. This gift is used by believers all throughout the New Testament to comfort those who are under pressure, to bring encouragement to people's hearts, and to redirect individual's attention back to God.

First Corinthians 14:3 says, "But he that prophesieth speaketh unto men to edification, and exhortation, and comfort." Here, Paul lets us know that the primary objective of prophecy is to impart edification, exhortation, and comfort to the listeners. When a person moves in this spiritual gift, he or she is divinely inspired to speak on behalf of God and to deliver a message that God wants to convey to His people at a particular moment or for a particular situation.

The operation of the gift of prophecy results in an individual or a congregation receiving new understanding about a truth, insight, or directive from the heart of God that helps strengthen, encourage, and instruct the listeners so they can walk with Him more accurately. An example of this gift in action is found in Acts 13 where we find that the elders of the church in Antioch were gathered together, fasting and praying before the Lord. Acts 13:2 says, "As they ministered to the Lord, and fasted, the Holy Ghost said, Separate me Barnabas and Saul for the work whereunto I have called them."

According to this verse, the gift of prophecy was at work as the Holy Spirit spoke through someone in the group and revealed the heart of the Spirit concerning Paul and Barnabas. Through that divine word, the Lord launched these two men out into their apostolic ministries. That is an example of the simple gift of prophecy, and the Bible says we can all prophesy and should seek this gift. As with all the gifts of the Spirit, God intends the gift of prophecy to operate in the Church until Jesus returns.

Discerning of Spirits

The next gift listed in First Corinthians 12:10 is *discerning of spirits*. The word "discerning" is the Greek word *diakrisis*, which means *distinguishing*, *perceiving*, or *discerning*. The word "spirits" is a translation of the Greek word *pneumaton*. It is plural, and it refers to *spirits* or *spiritual situations*. When these words are joined together to form the phrase "discerning of spirits," it means *to perceive things that are spiritual*. Hence the gift of "discerning of spirits" is the supernatural ability to read or perceive the true nature of a situation and discern what spiritual forces are really at work in a person's life or a certain situation.

This revelatory gift is a supernatural revealing — or discerning — of spiritual forces that cannot be naturally discerned, and it manifests in an instant. It's as though a curtain has suddenly been pulled back, and one is enabled to see into the spirit realm to know what is really happening behind the scenes — or to see or perceive the genuine spiritual condition that is otherwise hidden to the eyes.

The *discerning of spirits* is a vital piece of spiritual equipment, and it often manifests in spiritual leaders, as they need to spiritually perceive what kind of spiritual influences people are yielding to. The Holy Spirit also uses this gift to help leaders in the selection of a leadership team and to accurately see the true nature of a spiritual environment.

An example of this gift is found in Matthew's gospel when Jesus spoke to a man who was sick with palsy and said to him, "…Son, be of good cheer; thy sins be forgiven thee" (Matthew 9:2). In that moment, the Bible says, "…Certain of the scribes said within themselves, This man blasphemeth" (Matthew 9:3).

In the natural, it appeared these scribes were open and listening to Jesus, but Jesus knew otherwise. Suddenly, He supernaturally discerned what He could have never naturally known. The Bible says, "And Jesus *knowing their thoughts* said, Wherefore think ye evil in your hearts?" (Matthew 9:4) Although these scribes tried to conceal their true feelings, the gift of *discerning of spirits* enabled Jesus to supernaturally perceive what was occurring inside them and see the actual spiritual forces He was up against. This same powerful gift of the Spirit is available to you!

Divers Kinds of Tongues

Along with the gift of *prophecy* and *discerning of spirits*, another spiritual gift that Paul said has been distributed to the Church is *divers kinds of tongues* (1 Corinthians 12:10). The word "tongues" in this verse is the Greek word *glossa*, and it describes *tongues* or *languages*. It is where we get the word *glossolalia*.

It's important to note that the gift of *tongues* described by Paul in First Corinthians 12:10 is a public gift that is to be used for the edification or strengthening of the Church, and it's different from a devotional tongue that one uses in prayer. In the context of this passage, Paul was explicitly referring to that moment when someone is moved supernaturally by the Holy Spirit's prompting to deliver a specific message in tongues from the heart of God to an individual or to an assembled group.

And according to First Corinthians 14:5, Paul taught that when a public message in tongues is interpreted, it brings supernatural edification to the church. That's why the devil is against it. Some try to discount this particular gift as being less important, but Paul listed it right here alongside of all the other spiritual gifts — ranking it equal in importance to all the others.

Interpretation of Tongues

The final gift of the Spirit Paul includes in First Corinthians 12:10 is inseparable to the gift of *tongues*, and it is the *interpretation of tongues*. In Greek, the word "interpretation" is *hermeneia*, which describes *an interpretation of a public message in tongues*. Understand that this gift is not the "translation of tongues," rather the *interpretation of tongues*.

One who moves in this gift supernaturally understands and speaks out the meaning of a message in tongues that has been spoken, giving the gist of a message rather than a translation. In other words, the interpretation is an equivalent meaning and not a word-for-word rendering. This person may not understand what was said in tongues word for word, but he or she supernaturally has the ability to understand the essence of what the Holy Spirit is saying and to interpret it.

Keep in mind because it is an interpretation and not a translation, the length of the interpretation may not necessarily match the length of the message in tongues. Again, an interpretation is not a word-for-word translation. The gift of *interpretation of tongues* works in partnership with the public message of tongues, which is called *divers kinds of tongues* in Scripture.

An example of the interpretation of tongues and the gift of tongues would be found in First Corinthians 14 where Paul writes a long discussion about spiritual gifts and expounds upon speaking in *tongues* and the *interpretation of tongues*, giving explicit instructions on how to operate in these gifts. The church at Corinth had the gift of *divers kinds of tongues* in regular manifestation, so Paul wrote to help guide and instruct them how to properly flow in this gift as well as in the gift of *interpretation of tongues*. If you want to understand more about the operation of *tongues* and *interpretation of tongues*, please read First Corinthians 14.

A Few Final Thoughts About Spiritual Gifts

Always keep in mind that the gifts of the Spirit often work in pairs or in groupings. For example, where the *working of miracles* is manifesting, it is often accompanied by the gift of special *faith*. These two gifts working together can move mountains of opposition that literally are impossible to move in the natural realm.

Likewise, when the *word of knowledge* is in operation, it is often accompanied by the *gifts of healing* and the *working of miracles*. The variety of how these spiritual gifts work together in concert is diverse, but it is helpful to realize that whenever one of these spiritual gifts operates, it often does so in partnership with one or more of the other gifts.

Friend, we need the gifts of the Holy Spirit fully operating in our lives and in our churches today — to build and strengthen the Body of Christ and to bring the living person of Jesus right in our midst. Let's open our hearts and make room for the Holy Spirit to make His presence conspicuous in our midst!

STUDY QUESTIONS

Study to shew thyself approved unto God, a workman that needeth not to be ashamed, rightly dividing the word of truth.
— 2 Timothy 2:15

1. Are the gifts of the Holy Spirit in manifestation in your church? If not, do you know the reason why? Are you aware of what your pastor and church leaders believe about the gifts of the Spirit? Is the manifestation of the gifts permitted?

2. What spiritual gifts do *you* bring to the table? How are you managing the gifts God has given you?

3. God wants you to experience and flow in the gifts of the Holy Spirit. As the Spirit moves on you with His gifts, it is crucial to maintain a humble heart. Take a few moments and reflect on Paul's words in Romans 12:3-10 and First Corinthians 4:7. What wisdom can you take from these passages and apply to your life concerning the gifts of the Spirit?

PRACTICAL APPLICATION

But be ye doers of the word, and not hearers only, deceiving your own selves.
—James 1:22

1. As you heard about the gift of *prophecy*, *discerning of spirits*, *tongues*, and *interpretation of tongues*, what new insights did you learn? Out of the nine gifts of the Holy Spirit, which one (or ones) excite you and captivate you most? Why?

2. Have you ever been the recipient of the gift of *prophecy*? If so, what was the prophecy, and how did God use it in your life?

3. Take a moment to reflect on the gift of *discerning of spirits*. What benefits might this powerful gift provide you when it comes to being able to discern the spirits of those influencing you and your family? What is the detriment of not having this gift operating in your life?

4. Be honest. Have the gift of *tongues* and the gift of *interpretation of tongues* ever made you anxious or fearful? How about confused? If so, how has this lesson helped to bring clarity and peace to you regarding these gifts?

LESSON 8

TOPIC

Making Room for Spiritual Gifts

SCRIPTURES

1. **1 Corinthians 12:1** — Now concerning spiritual gifts, brethren, I would not have you ignorant.

2. **1 Corinthians 12:7** — But the manifestation of the Spirit is given to every man to profit withal.

3. **1 Corinthians 14:1** — Follow after charity [love], and desire spiritual gifts....

4. **1 Corinthians 1:7** — So that ye come behind in no gift; waiting for the coming of our Lord Jesus Christ.

5. **1 Corinthians 14:26** — How is it then, brethren? when ye come together, every one of you hath a psalm, hath a doctrine, hath a tongue, hath a revelation, hath an interpretation. Let all things be done unto edifying.

6. **1 Corinthians 14:12** — Even so ye, forasmuch as ye are zealous of spiritual gifts, seek that ye may excel to the edifying of the church.

7. **1 Corinthians 14:40** — Let all things be done decently and in order.

GREEK WORDS

1. "ignorant" — **ἀγνοέω** (*agnoeo*): ignorance; not to know; sometimes with the idea of willful ignorance
2. "manifestation" — **φανέρωσις** (*phanerosis*): apparent; appear; manifest; visible; something that is seen; conspicuous; observable; obvious; clear; open; apparent or evident
3. "every man" — **ἕκαστος** (*hekastos*): an all-inclusive term that embraces everyone, with no one excluded
4. "profit" — **συμφέρω** (*sumphero*): a joint or shared benefit; always profitable
5. "desire" — **ζηλόω** (*zeloo*): enthusiasm; fervor; passion; devotion; an eagerness to achieve or to possess something; to be fervently boiling with zealousness for the object desired; an intense desire that causes one to seek something until it is obtained
6. "come behind" — **ὑστερέω** (*hustereo*): behind and therefore left out; left wanting; falling short; insufficiency; a lack or a falling short of something and represents a deficiency or a coming behind; insufficiency that causes one to be inferior
7. "gift" — **χάρισμα** (*charisma*): from **χάρις** (*charis*) the word for grace; here it is a form of **χάρισμα** (*charisma*), which is a grace-imparted enablement
8. "every one" — **ἕκαστος** (*hekastos*): an all-inclusive term that embraces everyone, with no one excluded
9. "edifying" — **οἰκοδομή** (*oikodome*): an architectural term meaning to enlarge or amplify a house; it depicts the careful following of an architectural plan to enlarge, increase or amplify; to edify; to improve; to leave in an improved condition

SYNOPSIS

There's another interesting and relatively unknown fact about the Cathedral of Peter and Paul in the city of Saint Petersburg, Russia. Originally, it was intended to be the burial place for the entire Romanov family — from the start of the reign of Peter the Great to the present day. And because they wanted to make sure that there was enough room to accommodate all the Romanovs and their treasures, the cathedral was built substantially large.

Making room for who and what is most valuable and precious to us is very important. What are you doing to make room for the presence and power of the Holy Spirit? Are you creating adequate space for Him and His grace to move and manifest in and through your life? The Bible says, "…The Spirit Whom He [God] has caused to dwell in us yearns over us and He yearns for the Spirit [to be welcome] with a jealous love" (James 4:5 *AMPC*). If you will make room for the Holy Spirit, He will respond by releasing the fullness of His gifts in your life!

The emphasis of this lesson:

Spiritual gifts are vital to bring the supernatural dimension of Jesus Christ into the Church. We are not to merely want or wish for the gifts. We are to zealously desire and seek them, making room for the Holy Spirit to move in our lives and in our churches. The gifts of the Spirit are grace-imparted enablements, and we can never have too many.

God Wants You To Experience and Be Fully Aware of the Spiritual Gifts

The apostle Paul began his teaching on the gifts of the Holy Spirit by saying, "Now concerning spiritual gifts, brethren, I would not have you ignorant" (1 Corinthians 12:1). The word "ignorant" here is the Greek word *agnoeo*, which describes *ignorance* or *not knowing something*. In some cases, the word *agnoeo* carries the idea of *willful ignorance*. In other words, Paul is saying, "I do not want you to *not know* about the gifts of the Holy Spirit — either knowingly or unknowingly."

Paul went on to say, "…The manifestation of the Spirit is given to every man to profit withal" (1 Corinthians 12:7). We've seen that the word "manifestation" is the Greek word *phanerosis*, and it describes *something apparent, visible,* or *something that is seen*. It indicates *something conspicuous, observable, obvious, clear, open,* or *evident*. The use of this word lets us know that God wants the operation of the gifts of the Holy Spirit in our lives and in our churches to be *clear, obvious,* and *apparent* to all.

And God doesn't just want this for church leaders or for a select few. He said, "…The Spirit is given to every man…" (1 Corinthians 12:7). The words "every man" in Greek are a translation of the word *hekastos*, which is an all-inclusive term that embraces *everyone, with no one excluded*. This means if you have been born again by the Spirit of God and call Jesus your Lord and Savior, you are included in this verse! God wants the work of the Holy Spirit and the manifestation of His gifts to be obvious and observable in *your* life.

Why have the gifts of the Spirit been given? Paul said to "profit" every single believer. This word "profit" is the Greek word *sumphero*, and it describes *a joint or shared benefit; something that is always profitable*. The fact is there is nothing negative about the genuine manifestation of the gifts of the Holy Spirit. When they are in operation, they bring a shared benefit to the Body of Christ and to every believer.

It Is *Right* To Seek Spiritual Gifts

Now maybe you have heard someone say that it is wrong to seek spiritual gifts, but that is not true. If the gifts of the Holy Spirit are from God — and they are — why would it be wrong to seek them? If they really are God-given manifestations of the Spirit, shouldn't we desire them to work in us and among us? The answer is a resounding *yes*!

Please realize that Paul never rebuked or corrected the Corinthian believers for having so many spiritual gifts or for seeking their manifestation. On the contrary, he told them, "Follow after charity [love] and desire spiritual gifts..." (1 Corinthians 14:1). Although most Christians believe we are to follow after love, they have a tendency to overlook the second part of this verse. Yes, we are to *follow after love*, but we are also to *desire spiritual gifts*. These instructions are equally important.

The word "desire" here is the Greek word *zeloo*, and it describes *enthusiasm, fervor, passion*, and *devotion*. It depicts *an eagerness to achieve or to possess something; to be fervently boiling with zealousness for the object desired*. Moreover, this word *zeloo* — translated here as "desire" — denotes *an intense desire that causes one to seek something until it is obtained*. So when Paul says, "Desire spiritual gifts," he is saying, "Seek the manifestation of the gifts of the Holy Spirit until you have them in your grasp and they are operating in your life."

Clearly, Paul is not telling us to merely *want* or *wish* for the gifts. He is painting a picture of an intense longing and craving for the gifts. It is the image of one boiling over with zealousness to take hold of and experience these supernatural manifestations and walk in the deeper dimension of the Holy Spirit. Paul knew spiritual gifts were vital to bring the supernatural dimension of Christ to the Church, and that is why he really wanted the Corinthian Christians to *fervently boil with desire* and *to seek* for them.

You Can Never Have Too Many Gifts

So, if it's right to seek and earnestly desire spiritual gifts, you may be thinking, *How many gifts of the Holy Spirit are too many?* The answer to this question is found in First Corinthians 1:7, where Paul says, "So that ye come behind in no gift; waiting for the coming of our Lord Jesus Christ."

Notice the words "come behind." They are a translation of the Greek word *hustereo*, which means *behind and therefore left out* or *left wanting*. It carries the idea of *falling short, insufficiency, a lack,* or *a falling short of something*. It represents *a deficiency* or *a coming behind; an insufficiency that causes one to feel inferior.*

Normally, this word *hustereo* pictures a person or group of people that is inferior in comparison to others — or even depleted of whatever is needed and therefore insufficient to meet the needs that are presented to them. In this case, however, Paul did not use the word *hustereo* by itself. Instead, he included it with the word "not," which means he was telling the church at Corinth they were *not* inferior, *not* falling behind, and *not* deficient to other churches with respect to having the gifts of the Spirit.

On the contrary, in First Corinthians 1:7, Paul emphatically stated that the Corinthians were superior when it came to spiritual manifestations. These believers were so abundantly blessed in regard to the gifts of the Holy Spirit that Paul affirmed they were *second to none* in this respect. In fact, Paul's words in First Corinthians 1:7 tell us the church in Corinth had more supernatural spiritual manifestations in operation than any other church. If a conference had been held in the first century to teach on the gifts of the Holy Spirit, it probably would have been conducted in Corinth, because no church had more gifts or understanding about how to operate in the gifts of the Spirit than the Corinthian church. They were simply the premier example when it came to this subject.

The Gifts of the Spirit Are
'Grace-Imparted Enablements'

Another important word in First Corinthians 1:7 is the word "gift." Paul said, "So that ye come behind in no *gift*; waiting for the coming of our Lord Jesus Christ." In this verse, the word "gift" is the Greek word *charisma*, which is derived from the word *charis*, the word for *grace*. When the word *charis* becomes *charisma*, it is no longer *grace*, but it is *grace-imparted enablements*.

Interestingly, the word *charisma* is where we get the word *charismatic*. Those who call themselves by this name believe in the gifts of the Holy Spirit and believe the gifts have been imparted to them, or at least that they place a significant emphasis on the gifts of the Spirit in their expression of worship.

In any case, the word *charisma* was used to describe that moment when the gods graced or donated supernatural ability, favor, or power to an individual. Thus, this word *charisma* meant a *gracious gift* — and that is exactly how it should be interpreted in the New Testament. A person who has had a *charisma* imparted to him or her has received a donation or an enablement from God that equips that person in some supernatural manner.

Paul's words in First Corinthians 1:7 tell us that every known gift of the Holy Spirit was in manifestation in the Corinthian congregation. That is why he said that they "came behind in no gift." The Corinthian believers were simply *overflowing* with these demonstrations of the Spirit. This is what God wants for His entire Church and all His children — including *you*!

All Spiritual Manifestations
Are for the Purpose of 'Edifying'

When we come to First Corinthians 14:26, the apostle Paul gives us a sneak peek into what a church service was like in the church in Corinth. He said, "How is it then, brethren? when ye come together, every one of you hath a psalm, hath a doctrine, hath a tongue, hath a revelation, hath an interpretation. Let all things be done unto edifying."

First of all, Paul said, "When you all come together, every one of you brings something to the service." The word "every one" is once again the Greek word *hekastos*, an all-inclusive term that embraces *everyone*, *with no one excluded*. This means every single member of the Corinthian congregation moved in the manifestations of the Holy Spirit — *no one was excluded* in demonstrating the gifts.

It's also important to note that Paul did not correct or rebuke the believers for their abundance of gifts. It was not a problem that one had a psalm, one had a doctrine, one had a tongue, one had a revelation, and one had an interpretation. The only instruction that Paul gave the believers was to "…Let all things be done unto edifying" (1 Corinthians 14:26).

The word "edifying" here is quite remarkable. It is also found in First Corinthians 14:12, where Paul said, "Even so ye, forasmuch as ye are zealous of spiritual gifts, seek that ye may excel to the *edifying* of the church." In Greek, the word "edifying" in both verses is the word *oikodome*, which is an architectural term meaning *to enlarge or amplify a house*. It depicts the careful following of an architectural plan to enlarge, increase, or amplify the capacity of a structure. This word *oikodome* —translated in these verses as "edifying"— can also mean *to edify, to improve*, or *to leave in an improved condition*.

Think about it. When a person decides to construct a new room on his house — enlarging and improving his home — first he settles on a design. Once the plan is determined, it is carefully followed as the addition to the house is built little by little and the designer's dreams are realized.

By specifically choosing this word "edifying" — the Greek architectural term *oikodome* — Paul emphasized that **we must make room for the Holy Spirit to move among us.** As we allow the Spirit to work in the midst of us, **the gifts will spiritually enlarge us** and improve our ability to walk in the power of the Spirit.

Therefore, according to First Corinthians 14:12, the manifestation of the gifts of the Holy Spirit renovates our lives and leaves us in a better condition. When the gifts of the Spirit are in operation, it blasts out the walls, enlarges our spiritual capacity, and improves us, enabling us to walk in the *dunamis* power of God. Paul says we are to seek these spiritual gifts that we may excel in "edifying" the Church.

The only regulation or rule Paul established concerning the flow of spiritual gifts in the Church is found in First Corinthians 14:40, which says: "Let all things be done decently and in order." This will be the focus of our study for the next lesson.

STUDY QUESTIONS

Study to shew thyself approved unto God, a workman that needeth not to be ashamed, rightly dividing the word of truth.
— 2 Timothy 2:15

1. In Greek, the word "gift" is *charisma*, and it describes a *grace-imparted enablement*. What forms of *charisma* has the Holy Spirit imparted to you? What divine donation or enablement of God's power have you received, and what has it supernaturally equipped you to do?

2. How have the gifts of the Spirit *spiritually enlarged* you and improved your ability to walk in the power of the Spirit? How have they *renovated* your life and left you in a better condition?

3. The primary purpose of the gifts of the Spirit is found in First Corinthians 14:26: "...Let all things be done unto *edifying*." What else does God's Word say about *edifying* each other?

    • **Romans 14:19** and **1 Peter 3:11**

    • **1 Corinthians 8:1** and **1 Corinthians 13:4-8**

    • **Ephesians 4:29** and **Colossians 4:6**

    • **Ephesians 4:11-13**

PRACTICAL APPLICATION

But be ye doers of the word, and not hearers only, deceiving your own selves.
— James 1:22

1. Be honest: Have you been "willfully ignorant" about spiritual gifts and how they operate? If so, *who* or *what* have you been afraid of? How is this series helping to break fear off your life?

2. Through Paul, God says, "Follow after love and desire spiritual gifts..." (1 Corinthians 14:1). Be honest: Are you desiring spiritual gifts — are you *enthusiastically*, *passionately*, and *intensely pursuing* the manifesta-

tion of the gifts in your life? If not, why? What practical steps can you take to begin "desiring" the gifts of the Holy Spirit?

3. What are you doing to make room for the presence and power of the Holy Spirit in your life, in your family, and in your church? Pause and pray, *Lord, what can I begin to do to create even more space for You to move and manifest Your grace in and through my life?* Be still and listen. What is the Holy Spirit saying to you?

LESSON 9

TOPIC

The Need To Do Things Decently and in Order

SCRIPTURES

1. **1 Corinthians 12:1** — Now concerning spiritual gifts, brethren, I would not have you ignorant.

2. **1 Corinthians 14:40** — Let all things be done decently and in order.

3. **Romans 13:13** — Let us walk honestly, as in the day; not in rioting and drunkenness, not in chambering and wantonness, not in strife and envying.

4. **1 Thessalonians 4:12** — That ye may walk honestly toward them that are without, and that ye may have lack of nothing.

5. **1 Corinthians 14:29-33** — Let the prophets speak two or three, and let the other judge. If any thing be revealed to another that sitteth by, let the first hold his peace. For ye may all prophesy one by one, that all may learn, and all may be comforted. And the spirits of the prophets are subject to the prophets. For God is not the author of confusion, but of peace, as in all churches of the saints.

GREEK WORDS

1. "ignorant" — ἀγνοέω (*agnoeo*): ignorance; not to know; sometimes with the idea of willful ignorance

2. "decently" — εὐσχημόνως (*euschemonos*): honestly; pictures respect or honor; something done properly as opposed to improperly; only other usages are in Romans 13:13 and First Thessalonians 4:12

3. "honestly" — εὐσχημόνως (*euschemonos*): honestly; pictures respect or honor; something done properly as opposed to improperly

4. "order" — τάξις (*taksis*): something done in a fitting way or carried out according to order; depicted the orderly way in which the Roman army erected their camps, indicating their camps were orderly, organized, well-planned, and not hastily thrown together, but set up in an organized and thoughtful manner; used to picture people who were respectful, deferential, courteous, accommodating, well-mannered, and polite

SYNOPSIS

The Romanov family ruled the Russian Empire for 300 years, all the way up until the Bolshevik Revolution in 1917. During the cold, harsh winters, they spent their days in what is known as the Winter Palace in Saint Petersburg, Russia, which was and still is breathtaking in beauty. Inside this magnificent fortress, which is about the size of 12 football fields, there is a fully functioning church called the Great Church of the Winter Palace.

Although this church fell into disrepair over the years and was closed for a time, it was eventually totally renovated and reopened for use. Today, its interiors are just as beautiful as it ever was — decked out with magnificent ornamentation and embellished with more than 11 pounds of gold. There is even a priest that serves and presents a full liturgy for attendees, and everything done in this church is done decently and in order.

In the same way that things are conducted in the Great Church of the Winter Palace, God desires to do things in His Church. When Paul wrote to the church in Corinth and gave them direction about the flow of the gifts of the Spirit in their meetings, he gave them only one rule: "Let all things be done decently and in order" (1 Corinthians 14:40). This was and still is the heart of God concerning the manifestations of the Holy Spirit in the Church.

The emphasis of this lesson:

God wants *all the gifts* of the Holy Spirit manifesting in your life and in His Church — *decently and in order*. Although this guideline means different things to different people, essentially the words *decently and in order* mean we exercise the gifts of the Spirit honestly and properly, being respectful and doing things in a well-mannered, organized way.

Don't Be Ignorant of the Gifts

When it came to spiritual gifts, the church in Corinth was like no other church in the First Century. Paul said they came behind or were deficient in no gifts (*see* 1 Corinthians 1:7). And yet, with all their experience and an overflow of spiritual manifestations, Paul told the Corinthians, "Now concerning spiritual gifts, brethren, I would not have you ignorant" (1 Corinthians 12:1). This word "ignorant" is the Greek word *agnoeo*, which describes *ignorance* or *not knowing something*. In some cases, the word *agnoeo* carries the idea of *willful ignorance*.

The truth is sometimes believers are willfully ignorant about the gifts of the Holy Spirit because they're afraid to talk about it. They are fearful of how others may respond if they desire to see Him operate in the Church and open the door to the manifestations of the Spirit. But God did not give the gifts of the Holy Spirit to frighten anyone. He gave us the gifts of the Spirit to bring the supernatural reality of Jesus to the Church.

When Paul said, "Now concerning spiritual gifts, brethren, I would not have you ignorant" (1 Corinthians 12:1), he was saying, "I don't want you to *not know* about the gifts of the Holy Spirit — either knowingly or unknowingly." Likewise, we are not supposed to be ignorant about spiritual gifts. We are to understand what they are, how they work, and know how to partner with the Spirit.

'Let *All Things* Be Done'

As we said in the introduction, there was only one rule Paul gave about flowing in the manifestation of spiritual gifts, and it's found in First Corinthians 14:40: "Let all things be done decently and in order." Before we get into understanding the meaning of the phrase "decently and in order," it is vital that we not miss the first part of what Paul said in this verse: "Let all things be done...."

Many Christians become so fixated on the words "decently and in order" that they overlook the fact that when it comes to spiritual gifts operating in the Church, we are to "Let all things be done." God wants *all the gifts* of the Holy Spirit manifesting in your life and in His Church. So make room for it all! Don't worry about having too many manifestations. You can make room for all of them. The only guideline or stipulation God gave through Paul is, "Let all things be done decently and in order" (1 Corinthians 14:40).

Differing Backgrounds Produce Differing Opinions

The words "decently and in order" mean different things to different people. What is acceptable to one group may be outrageous and offensive to another group. Likewise, what is deemed holy, sweet, and touching to one person may be viewed as dead, dull, and monotonous to another. Everyone has his own opinions about what is appropriate or inappropriate in worship.

The fact is, the Body of Christ is composed of Catholics, Orthodox Christians, Baptists, Methodists, Episcopalians, Pentecostals, and Charismatics, and we're all affected by our past denominational backgrounds. Depending on what group you are from, it will likely flavor what you believe is right and wrong about what is done in church or what you believe is considered "decently and in order."

You may personally believe that praise and worship with instruments, clapping, dancing, and all kinds of celebration is the right approach. Having drums, brass instruments, and electric guitars woven into worship is what you've come to know and embrace as commonplace. Or you may be a person who loves a quieter, more traditional and structured form of worship with hymns and organ music. The truth is, there will be times when it is appropriate to enjoy a lively celebration in God's presence, and there will also be times when your heart is drawn to a quieter, deeper time of sacred worship. It all depends on the moving of the Holy Spirit in each particular gathering.

So don't be surprised that Christians have differing opinions about the right and the wrong way to worship God. Most people assume that their form of worship is the most scriptural. That said, and the fact that there are so many different opinions, who is right and who is wrong? What does

God actually mean when He says, "Let all things be done decently and in order"? (1 Corinthians 14:40).

We Are Called To Do Things 'Decently'

When it comes to the New Testament, only one basic rule is given to the Church to follow regarding this question of what is acceptable and appropriate in church services: "Let all things be done decently and in order" (1 Corinthians 14:40). The word "decently" in this verse is the Greek word *euschemonos*, and it basically describes something done *honestly*. It pictures *respect* or *honor* and describes *something done properly* as opposed to improperly.

What's interesting is that this word *euschemonos*, which is translated "decently" in First Corinthians 14:40, is translated as the word "honestly" in Romans 13:13 and First Thessalonians 4:12. In Romans 13:13, Paul said, "Let us walk *honestly*, as in the day; not in rioting and drunkenness, not in chambering and wantonness, not in strife and envying."

The word "honestly" in this verse is again the Greek word *euschemonos*, which pictures *respect* or *honor* and describes *something done properly* as opposed to improperly. In the context of this passage, the word "honestly" carries the idea of living respectfully, living culturally, being polite to others, doing things properly as opposed to doing things improperly, which means we are to be proper, polite, and cultured in our church setting. Therefore, when the Holy Spirit is moving in a loud, lively way, He will not be rude, lewd, or disrespectful, and neither should we. We can be loud and high-spirited and still do it in a very polite, spiritually cultural way.

In First Thessalonians 4:12, Paul speaks a similar sentiment saying, "That ye may walk *honestly* toward them that are without, and that ye may have lack of nothing." The word "honestly" here is again the Greek word *euschemonos*, which depicts *respect* or *honor* and describes *something done properly* as opposed to improperly. Once again, it is a picture of us being cultured, polite, and proper with others.

Yes, we need to surrender to the Holy Spirit and do what He tells us to do, but whatever the Spirit tells us to do in a church service should always be done "decently." God is a God of order. He's not rude, uncivilized, or coarse. He is very proper, gracious, and cultured Himself, and He always requires us to manifest spiritual gifts in a decent, cultured, proper, polite way.

We Are Called To Do Things 'In Order'

Now that we have nailed down the meaning of the word "decently," what exactly do the words "in order" mean? Paul said, "Let all things be done decently and *in order*"? (1 Corinthians 14:40). The word "order" here is a translation of the Greek word *taksis*, which describes *something done in a fitting way or carried out according to order.*

This very word was used by the Jewish historian Josephus to depict the orderly way in which the Roman army erected their camps, indicating that their camps were orderly, organized, well-planned, and not hastily thrown together. The commanders didn't engage in last-minute planning. They had their troops set up in an organized and thoughtful manner.

Josephus also used the word *taksis* — translated as "order" — to describe the way Essene Jews were respectful of others. These Jews would wait until others were finished speaking before they'd take their turn to speak out. They didn't interrupt one another. Thus, this word *taksis* pictures people who were *respectful, deferential, courteous, accommodating, well-mannered,* and *polite.*

Taking into account the original Greek meaning of the words "decently and in order," here is the *Renner Interpretive Version (RIV)* of First Corinthians 14:40:

> **Let everything be done in a respectful, fitting and proper manner that is organized, well-planned, respectful, well-mannered, and polite.**

This lets us know that a service can be quiet, loud, soft, or bold. The important thing is that everything is done properly, respectfully, and in an organized fashion. This includes the time of worship. Neither worship nor anything else should be thrown together at the last minute with no thought or organization. After all, we're talking about believers coming together to worship Almighty God.

At the same time, it's important for us to leave room for the Holy Spirit to "change things up" spontaneously if He desires. Our ultimate goal should always be to **follow His order**, whatever that looks like in a given situation. Of course, when believers come together, all who participate should be well-mannered, respectful, and polite.

The big question in God's mind is: *What is our intent and heart motivation?* If a group's intent and motivation is correct, their worship will be accompanied by an attitude that reflects the character of Jesus Christ. So don't get upset if others do things a little differently than the way you are accustomed to worshiping. Their form may be different than yours, but if they are worshiping God from pure hearts and with their entire being, you can rest assured that their worship is acceptable to Jesus.

The Proper Way of Handling Multiple Manifestations of the Spirit in One Meeting

Someone may ask, "When it comes to spiritual gifts operating in a local church, how many are too many?" Well, since they are the gifts of the Holy Spirit, this would be like asking, "How much of the Holy Spirit is too much?" The answer, of course, is we want *all* that the Holy Spirit has to give us!

One thing is certain: If the Holy Spirit is manifesting multiple gifts in a service, He is not going to move on believers to interrupt one another. That's just not the way He works, which is why He prompted the apostle Paul to give us one simple rule in First Corinthians 14:40: "Let all things be done decently and in order."

To make sure we understand the Holy Spirit's desires, Paul gives us this specific example of what should and shouldn't take place in a worship service:

> **Let the prophets speak two or three, and let the other judge. If any thing be revealed to another that sitteth by, let the first hold his peace. For ye may all prophesy one by one, that all may learn, and all may be comforted. And the spirits of the prophets are subject to the prophets. For God is not the author of confusion, but of peace, as in all churches of the saints.**
> **— 1 Corinthians 14:29-33**

In this passage, Paul recognized that a multiplicity of manifestations may occur in a single meeting, and that is okay. He encouraged the Corinthians — *and us* — to manifest all the gifts. He simply asked that those who spoke by the Spirit would refrain from interrupting others before they were finished. Remember, "…God is not the author of confusion, but of peace…" (1 Corinthians 14:33).

Also notice Paul said, "...The spirits of the prophets are subject to the prophets" (1 Corinthians 14:32). This means each believer has the ability to control himself. We don't have to raise our voice louder than someone else and interrupt them. Our motivation should never be to steal the show and get the attention and praises of people. All praise and glory belong to God.

Friend, we need the gifts of the Holy Spirit to operate among us. And in order to see these divine manifestations, we have to make room for it to happen. Many churches today have excelled at making room for people by creating multiple services for people to attend. But we can't be so focused on making room for people that we forget or ignore making room for the Holy Spirit.

If we will make room for the Holy Spirit and focus on learning how to more effectively allow Him to move, He will manifest His gifts among us, and He will teach us how to do it in a decent and orderly fashion.

STUDY QUESTIONS

Study to shew thyself approved unto God, a workman that needeth not to be ashamed, rightly dividing the word of truth.
— 2 Timothy 2:15

1. When it comes to manifesting spiritual gifts, God says, "Let all things be done decently and in order" (1 Corinthians 14:40). Prior to this lesson, had you noticed the first part of this verse — that God wants *all things* to be done? How does this revelation change your perspective on the gifts of the Spirit?

2. Carefully read Paul's instructions in First Corinthians 14:29-33 in a few different Bible versions. What is the Holy Spirit showing you in this passage regarding what should and shouldn't take place in a worship service? (Also consider James 3:13-17 and Psalm 133.)

3. Have you ever gotten upset with other believers because they worship and do things a little different than the way you are accustomed to doing them? That's actually what caused Cain to eventually rise up against Abel (*see* Genesis 4:1-8). According to Philippians 3:15 and 16, what can you always trust God to do? In the meantime, where should your focus be? (For a fuller understanding, check out these verses in a few different Bible versions.)

PRACTICAL APPLICATION

**But be ye doers of the word, and not hearers only,
deceiving your own selves.
— James 1:22**

1. Take a few moments and write down your honest opinion about what you believe is *appropriate* and *inappropriate* in worship — including the manifestations of the Holy Spirit.

2. Now, reflect on the meaning of the words "decently and in order." Would you say that the manifestation of the gifts of the Spirit in your church gatherings meet these requirements? If they do not, what is the Holy Spirit showing you that needs to change?

3. Prior to this lesson, what did you understand the phrase "decently and in order" in First Corinthians 14:40 to mean? How has this teaching made these words clearer to you regarding the manifestation of spiritual gifts in the Church?

LESSON 10

TOPIC

The Church of Corinth: A Divine Pattern or an Anomaly?

SCRIPTURES

1. **1 Corinthians 12:1** — Now concerning spiritual gifts, brethren, I would not have you ignorant.

2. **1 Corinthians 14:1** — Follow after charity [love], and desire spiritual gifts....

GREEK WORDS

1. "ignorant" — ἀγνοέω (*agnoeo*): ignorance; not to know; sometimes with the idea of willful ignorance

2. "desire" — ζηλόω (*zeloo*): enthusiasm; fervor; passion; devotion; an eagerness to achieve or to possess something; to be fervently boiling

with zealousness for the object desired; an intense desire that causes one to seek something until it is obtained

SYNOPSIS

As we noted in our previous lesson, the Winter Palace in Saint Petersburg, Russia, was the wintertime home of the Romanov family for many years, and it was simply an enormous facility. Over time, the building was expanded on several occasions, and if you were to measure the entire complex today, you would find it has 2,511,000 square feet — approximately the size of 12 football fields!

In the very heart of this remarkable fortress is the Great Church of the Winter Palace, which was designed by the famous Italian architect Francesco Rastrelli and completed in 1762. Its interiors are adorned with exquisite marble, precious stones, dazzling silver, and 11 pounds of glistening gold ornamentation on the walls. There is even a spectacular painting of the ascension of Jesus hallowing the ceiling.

All these marvelous physical embellishments bring to mind the spiritual embellishments God has given to us, His Church. A perfect example of this lavish provision is what God did in the church in Corinth. The Bible says the believers there lacked no spiritual gifts. As a matter of fact, Paul called them spiritual plutocrats — they were so stinking rich spiritually they couldn't count all the spiritual gifts God had given them. This brings us to a very important question: Was what happened in the church in Corinth an anomaly, or is it a pattern God intended to be duplicated in every church and in the life of every believer?

The emphasis of this lesson:

The New Testament is filled with explicit teaching and practical guidelines on the gifts of the Spirit and how they should operate in the Church. In fact, it addresses the operation of spiritual gifts nearly four times more than the subjects of water baptism and communion. This shows the vast importance God places on the manifestation of the Holy Spirit and signifies that what happened in Corinth is a pattern for all churches through all generations.

Don't Be Afraid To Learn About Spiritual Gifts

When Paul began his teaching on the gifts of the Spirit, he wrote to the Corinthians and said, "Now concerning spiritual gifts, brethren, I would not have you ignorant" (1 Corinthians 12:1). This statement is quite amazing because the believers Paul was writing to were abounding in the manifestation of the gifts of the Holy Spirit. Yet, he wanted them to know even more and not be ignorant about the gifts. The word "ignorant" in this verse is a form of the Greek word *ginosko*, which means *to know*. However, when an "a" is attached to the front of this word and it becomes *agnoeo*, the meaning is negated or reversed. Hence, the word *agnoeo* — "ignorant" — means *to not know*, and sometimes even carries with it the idea of *willful ignorance*.

Unfortunately, some people are willfully ignorant regarding the gifts of the Holy Spirit, and the reason for their ignorance is *fear*. They say things like, "Oh, I'm just afraid of talking about the Holy Ghost. That's just too radical for me." Or they say, "I'm afraid of what will happen in our church if we begin to move in the gifts of the Holy Spirit. What will newcomers think? How will we maintain control of the service?" So out of fear, they steer clear of the subject of spiritual gifts.

If you have adopted this line of thinking or have stayed away from learning about the gifts of the Spirit for some other reason, make a decision today to make an about-face and begin learning about the Holy Spirit and His supernatural manifestations.

How Important Is the Subject of the Gifts of the Spirit?

Most people would agree that the more the Bible talks about a subject, the more important that subject is. That being the case, let's take a few minutes to compare two other prominent Bible doctrines — the doctrines of **water baptism** and **communion** — with the doctrine of the **gifts of the Holy Spirit** and see just how much attention God gave to each topic.

For 2,000 years, the Church has practiced water baptism and communion. We hold these two practices as holy acts of faith. The question is, how much scriptural real estate did God give to these two ordinances of the Church? If you do a study to compare the quantity of verses about *spiritual gifts* in the New Testament with the number of verses about *water baptism* and *communion*, what you find will surprise you.

Take the doctrine of **water baptism**, for example. In the entire New Testament, there are 16 passages with 23 references that address the subject of water baptism. These references are:

Matthew 3:13-16; 28:19; Mark 16:16; Luke 3:7,21; 7:29; John 4:1; Acts 2:38-41; 8:12,13,38,39; 9:18; 10:48; 16:15,33; 19:5; Romans 6:3-5; 1 Corinthians 1:15-17; 15:29; Ephesians 4:5

Based on these 16 passages with 23 references, the Church has dogmatically taught water baptism for 2,000 years as a requirement for every true disciple of Jesus Christ. No one would question the importance of water baptism — even with a minimal number of verses that deal with the subject.

Now what makes this even more interesting is that out of the 23 references, there is not a single verse in the New Testament to tell us how to practically conduct this important act of faith. Imagine something so important as water baptism, yet we are given absolutely no practical instructions in the New Testament as to how we are to do it!

What about the subject of **communion**? Similarly, in the entire New Testament, there are only 7 passages with 28 references that address the subject of communion. These references are:

Matthew 26:26-29; Mark 14:22-25; Luke 22:19,20; John 13:2; Acts 2:42; 1 Corinthians 10:16-21; 11:23-33

In spite of the fact that there are only a few passages and references, we believe in communion and have practiced it with heartfelt faith and commitment for 2,000 years. No one would argue about its vital role in the Church since the Day of Pentecost.

That said, it seems logical to assume that since communion has such a significant purpose in the life of the Church, there would be verses in the New Testament committed to giving us practical instruction on how to serve and partake of communion. However, as in the case of water baptism, there are no practical guidelines on how to administrate communion.

What About the Subject of Spiritual Gifts?

If you count all the verses in the New Testament that address the subject of the **gifts of the Holy Spirit** — including the fivefold ministry gifts, the motivational gifts, and the nine gifts of the Spirit we are discussing in this series — and that also give concrete, well-established guidelines on how these gifts should operate in the Church, you'll discover there are **103 verses** that fit this description. These verses are:

Romans 1:11; 12:5-8; 1 Corinthians 1:5-9; 12:1-31; 13:1-13; 14:1-40; Ephesians 4:11-13; 1 Timothy 1:18; 4:14; 2 Timothy 1:6; Hebrews 2:4; 1 Peter 4:10,11

Clearly, the New Testament is filled with explicit teaching on the gifts of the Spirit, even providing practical guidelines on how the gifts of the Spirit should operate. For instance, First Corinthians 14 contains 40 verses devoted to practical instruction about how the gifts of the Spirit are to operate in your life and in the Church. Isn't that amazing! Look again at the comparison of the number of references addressing each of these doctrines of the Bible:

23 References About Water Baptism

28 References About Communion

103 References About Spiritual Gifts

And out of all the verses discussing water baptism and the verses discussing communion, there's not a single verse in the New Testament to give practical instruction on how to conduct these two major ordinances of the Church.

What Conclusions Can We Draw From These Comparisons?

Statistically, the New Testament addresses the operation of spiritual gifts **four times more** than the subject of water baptism and **almost four times more** than the subject of communion. This should speak volumes to us about the importance that God places on the gifts of the Holy Spirit and the role these gifts should have in the life of every believer and every congregation.

For the moment, let's put away any doctrinal preconceptions and look at this from a purely statistical, logical point of view. We would never question whether or not we are to practice water baptism and communion, right? We believe in these ordinances and practice them with deep reverence based on 23 and 28 biblical references respectively. Yet, people often "argue" that the gifts of the Spirit — which are statistically more prominent and referred to 103 times in the New Testament — are unnecessary or optional!

If people would simply look objectively at the number of scriptures that address spiritual gifts as compared to scriptures addressing water baptism and communion, they might very well reach the conclusion that the gifts of the Spirit should carry at least *equal importance* to these other two practices of the Church!

Friend, God is a good Steward of all things, including space in the New Testament! If the gifts of the Holy Spirit were going to "pass away" with the death of the apostles, as some teach — or if spiritual gifts were less important than these other subjects mentioned — why would God commit so much space in the New Testament to this topic? Is it totally illogical to think He would include so many verses on the gifts of the Spirit if He knew they were short-lived and would pass away?

The argument that the gifts of the Spirit passed away or that they are optional is nonsense. The fact is, God expects the gifts of the Spirit to be manifested in abundance in the Church for the duration of the Church Age. First Corinthians 1:7 says they are to be in demonstration until "…the coming of our Lord Jesus Christ."

God doesn't want us to just know Christ intellectually. On the contrary, He longs for Jesus to step off the pages of the New Testament right into the midst of our lives and our church gatherings. And that's one of the major reasons we need the manifestation of the gifts of the Holy Spirit. When the gifts are operating in our lives and in our churches, they bring the reality of Jesus to us and confirm that His testimony in God's Word is true. Therefore, we must open our hearts to the work of the Holy Spirit.

Are You Desiring Spiritual Gifts?

What the apostle Paul wrote to the Corinthian believers in First Corinthians 14:1 is also God's instruction for us: "Follow after love and desire spiritual gifts…" (1 Corinthians 14:1). Although most Christians believe the first part of the verse — that we are to follow after love — some disagree with the second part. Well, if the first part of the verse is true, then so is the second part. If we are to *follow after love*, then we are also to *desire spiritual gifts*. Both directives are equally important.

As we saw in our previous lesson, the word "desire" here is the Greek word *zeloo*, and it describes *enthusiasm, fervor, passion*, and *devotion*. It depicts *an eagerness to achieve or to possess something*. It means *to be fervently boiling with zealousness for the object desired*. Likewise, this word *zeloo* — translated here as "desire" — denotes *an intense desire that causes one to seek something until it is obtained*. This means when Paul said, "Desire spiritual gifts," he was saying, "Seek the manifestation of the gifts of the Holy Spirit *until they are obtained*."

Friend, if you're tired of the absence of the supernatural in your own life and tired of attending services where you don't see any miraculous manifestations of the Holy Spirit, then begin to actively *desire* and *pray* for spiritual gifts to operate in your life, in your church, and in the Body of Christ. Without question, it is God's will to bring this about. If you will passionately pursue the presence of the Holy Spirit and make room for His gifts, He will show up!

STUDY QUESTIONS

Study to shew thyself approved unto God, a workman that needeth not to be ashamed, rightly dividing the word of truth.
— 2 Timothy 2:15

1. In this lesson, we learned that there are 23 references in the Bible about water baptism and 28 references about communion, yet not one of these references provide practical instructions on how to baptize in water or administrate communion. Does this change in any way how you view or value water baptism or communion? Would the small number of verses about each of these church practices stop you from participating in and promoting them?

2. A careful study of Scripture reveals that it contains 103 references about spiritual gifts, which is *four times* more than the subject of water baptism and *almost four times* more than the subject of communion. How does this fact affect your perspective of the importance of learning about and operating in the gifts of the Holy Spirit?

3. According to First Timothy 4:14 and Second Timothy 1:6, what are you to continue doing with the spiritual gifts God has deposited in you? (Also consider First Peter 4:10,11; Ecclesiastes 9:10.)

PRACTICAL APPLICATION

**But be ye doers of the word, and not hearers only,
deceiving your own selves.
— James 1:22**

1. Given the information you've learned in this lesson, what might you respectfully say to those who often argue that the gifts of the Spirit are unnecessary or optional — even though they are statistically more prominent in the New Testament?

2. Are you tired of the absence of the supernatural in your own life and tired of attending services where you don't see any miraculous manifestations of the Holy Spirit? Then begin to actively *desire* and *pray* for spiritual gifts to operate in your life, in your church, and in the Body of Christ.

   Pray: *Father, forgive me and Your people for neglecting the study and practice of the gifts of the Spirit. And forgive us, Holy Spirit, for closing the door on You in our church services. We need You desperately in our lives, in our churches, and in our nation. Help us make room for You, Holy Spirit — personally and collectively. Please come and move in Your power, Your glory, and Your mighty gifts! Bring the living reality of Jesus into our midst. I ask this in Jesus' name. Amen.*

Notes

Notes

CPSIA information can be obtained
at www.ICGtesting.com
Printed in the USA
LVHW080922241121
704334LV00013B/339